Number SENSE

Simple Effective Number Sense Experiences

Grades 3–4

Alistair McIntosh

Barbara Reys

Robert Reys

DALE SEYMOUR PUBLICATIONS®

Project Editor: Joan Gideon

Production Coordinator: Leanne Collins

Art: Rachel Gage

Cover design: Lynda Banks

Text design: Nancy Benedict

Published by Dale Seymour Publications®, an imprint of the Alternative Publishing Group of Addison-Wesley Publishing Company.

Order Number DS21801

ISBN 1-57232-262-4

This book is printed on recycled paper.

1 2 3 4 5 6 7 8 9 10-ML-00 99 98 97 96

CONTENTS

INTRODUCTION

Number sense refers to a person's understanding of number concepts, operations, and applications of numbers and operations. It includes the ability and inclination to use this understanding in flexible ways to make mathematical judgments and to develop useful strategies for handling numbers and operations. Number sense results in an expectation that numbers are useful and that mathematics has a certain regularity. A person with good number sense has the ability to use numbers and quantitative methods to communicate, process, and interpret information.

The four-book *Number SENSE: Simple Effective Number Sense Experiences* series is designed to promote thinking and reflection about numbers. The activities help students in primary through middle grades develop number sense through exploring patterns, developing mental-computation skills, understanding different but equivalent representations, establishing benchmarks, recognizing reasonableness, and acquiring estimation skills. Visualization is integral to many activities, as number sense is often developed from visual experiences.

The six sections of this book explore the major components of number sense:

- **Exploring Mental Computation**
  Calculating exact answers mentally, and exploring the thinking that facilitates mental computation

- **Exploring Multiple Representation**
  Identifying and using equivalent forms of numbers and expressions

- **Exploring Number Relationships**
  Exploring number patterns and connections between numbers, and understanding the effect of an operation—addition, subtraction, multiplication, division—on two or more numbers

- **Exploring Relative Size**
  Developing a sense of the size of a number in relation to other numbers, including benchmarks

- **Exploring Estimation**
  Working with approximate values to calculate and estimate

- **Exploring Measurement**
  Establishing and working with benchmarks to facilitate estimation

Each activity falls under one appropriate heading, though most are connected to more than one component of number sense. These interconnections are natural and a reminder that number sense is not a series of disjoint entities but an integration of multidimensional components.

Using the Activities

Each activity is built on the premise that any student can benefit at any time from experiences that encourage them to think about numbers in a sense-making way. The activities can be used in any order, whenever they would be appropriate to anchor, build, and extend students' thinking about numbers in meaningful ways. Most will take from 5 to 15 minutes.

The activities are designed to serve as a source for questions or problems to stimulate thinking and discussion. If the activity is to be presented to the whole class, the activity master may be made into a transparency. Activity masters may also be used to make student copies. When an experience contains more than one activity, begin with the first activity and use the others over a period of time.

Teacher notes explain the intent of each group of activities and suggest ways to present them. The teacher notes contain these components:

- **Number Sense Focus**
  Highlights the main number sense components

- **Number Focus**
  Identifies the types of numbers used in the activity

- **Mathematical Background**
  Describes the rationale or context for the activity, including its connection to different dimensions of number sense—such as relationships of fractions, multiple representation, computational alternatives, and basic facts

- **Using the Activity**
  Offers ideas for preparing students for the activity as well as ways to initiate the experience, questions to raise, and possible directions to take.

- **Solutions**

  Provides answers when appropriate and additional insight for some answers

- **Extending the Activity**

  Suggests teacher-directed extensions or variations as well as extensions for students to explore on their own

The Importance of Number Sense

● ●

Current reforms in mathematics education emphasize number sense as it typifies the theme of learning mathematics as a sense-making activity. Like common sense, *number sense* is an elusive term. It has been discussed by mathematics educators, including classroom teachers, curriculum writers, and researchers. Discussions include lists of essential components of number sense (McIntosh, Reys, and Reys, 1992; Resnick, 1989; Sowder and Schappelle, 1989; Sowder, 1992; Willis, 1990), descriptions of students displaying number sense (or lack thereof) (Howden, 1989; Reys, 1991, 1994), and an in-depth theoretical analysis of number sense from a psychological perspective (Greeno, 1991). Number sense is highly personal. It is related to *what* ideas about number have been established as well as to *how* those ideas were established.

The NCTM *Curriculum and Evaluation Standards* sets forth that children with good number sense have well-understood number meanings, understand multiple interpretations and representations of numbers, recognize the relative and absolute magnitude of numbers, appreciate the effect of operations on numbers, and have developed a system of personal benchmarks.

Number sense exhibits itself in various ways as the learner engages in mathematical thinking. It is an important underlying theme as the learner chooses, develops, and uses computational methods, including written computation, mental computation, calculators, and estimation. The creation and application of algorithms calls upon facets of number sense such as decomposition, recomposition, and understanding number properties. When paper-and-pencil algorithms and calculator algorithms are used, number sense is important as answers are evaluated for reasonableness.

The acquisition of number sense is gradual, commencing long before formal schooling begins. Number sense is often evident at an early age as children try to make sense of numbers. However, growing older does not necessarily ensure either the development or use of even the most primitive notions of number sense. Indeed, although many young children exhibit creative and sometimes efficient strategies for operating with numbers, attention to formal algorithms may actually deter use of informal methods. As students' technical knowledge of mathematics expands, their range of strategies may narrow.

Learned algorithms become the methods most cherished by many students, as they can be executed without much thought. The reaction of a student when asked whether a calculation seems reasonable is often to recalculate—generally using the same method as before—rather than to reflect on the result in light of the context. The lack of a natural inclination to reconsider a calculation is all too common both in and out of school. When selling three items priced at $2.19 each, a clerk reported a total due of $4.88. When the customer responded that the amount seemed too low, the clerk showed no inclination to reflect on the reasonableness of the result. When pressed, the clerk recalculated the amount due. Only when a different total appeared on the register did the clerk recognize an error. While the method of checking (recalculating) is not being questioned, the lack of reflective reasoning is worrisome.

There is evidence that the context in which mathematical problems are encountered influences a student's thinking. For example, while a student may be comfortable in school with a sum of 514 produced by applying a learned algorithm to the computation of 26 + 38, the same student in a store will likely demand a reexamination if asked to pay $5.14 for two items priced at 26¢ and 38¢.

Students who are highly skilled at paper-and-pencil computations—often the gauge by which mathematics success is measured—may or may not be developing good number sense. When a student reports that $40 - 36 = 16$ or that $\frac{2}{5} + \frac{3}{7} = \frac{5}{12}$, he or she is attempting to apply a learned algorithm but is not reflecting on the reasonableness of the answer. In fact, much of the recent attention to developing number sense is a reaction to overemphasis on computational, algorithmic procedures.

The degree of number sense needed in the world today is greater than ever. Both students and adults encounter a greater range of numbers (government budgets in the trillions of dollars, athletic events timed to the thousandths of a second), in more varied contexts (including graphs and surveys), and encounter more tools (such as computers and calculators) than a generation ago. It might be said that the possession of number sense is the one major attribute that distinguishes human beings from computers. There is every reason to believe that the twenty-first century will demand an even higher level of number sense.

The Teacher's Role in Developing Number Sense

The breadth and depth of students' number sense will grow as they encounter situations that encourage them to reflect on reasonableness, to think about numbers and operations, and to make flexible use of numbers and operations in a variety of situations. Focusing on number sense encourages students to use common sense and to become involved in making sense of numerical situations. *Sense making* is what number sense is all about.

As a teacher, you play a key role in developing your students' number sense by encouraging them to make sense of situations. As activities are explored, spend plenty of time discussing answers and strategies by focusing on questions such as these:

- How did you get your answer?

- Can you explain it another way?

- Did anyone think about it differently?

When there are wrong answers, find out why. Was it faulty reasoning, a computational error, or something else? Sharing how people—including you—thought about the question or problem provides different dimensions of insight into the solution process.

The activities in this book encourage dialogue among students and teachers. We believe that the success of these activities in promoting sense making will be directly related to the quality of the sharing and exchanging of ideas that occurs in your classroom.

References

Greeno, J. G. "Number Sense as Situated Knowing in a Conceptual Domain." *Journal for Research in Mathematics Education* 22 (1991): 170–218.

Howden, H. "Teaching Number Sense." *The Arithmetic Teacher* 36 (1989): 6–11.

McIntosh, A., B. Reys, and R. Reys. "A Proposed Framework for Examining Basic Number Sense." *For the Learning of Mathematics* 12 (1992): 2–8.

National Council of Teachers of Mathematics. *Curriculum and Evaluation Standards for School Mathematics.* Reston, Va.: National Council of Teachers of Mathematics, 1989.

Resnick, L. B. "Defining, Assessing and Teaching Number Sense." In *Establishing Foundations for Research on Number Sense and Related Topics: Report of a Conference,* eds. J. Sowder and B. Schappelle. San Diego, Calif.: San Diego State University, Center for Research in Mathematics and Science Education, 1989.

Reys, B. J., R. Barger, B. Dougherty, J. Hope, L. Lembke, Z. Markovits, A. Parnas, S. Reehm, R. Sturdevant, M. Weber, and M. Bruckheimer. *Developing Number Sense in the Middle Grades.* Reston, Va.: NCTM, 1991.

Reys, B. J. "Promoting Number Sense in Middle Grades." *Mathematics Teaching in the Middle Grades* 1, no. 2 (1994): 114–20.

Sowder, J. T. "Estimation and Number Sense." In *Handbook of Research on Mathematics Teaching and Learning,* ed. D. A. Grouws, 371–89. New York: Macmillan, 1992.

Sowder J. T. and B. P. Schappelle, eds. *Establishing Foundations for Research on Number Sense and Related Topics: Report of a Conference.* San Diego, Calif.: San Diego State University, Center for Research in Mathematics and Science Education, 1989.

Willis, S., ed. *Being Numerate: What Counts?* Hawthorne, Victoria: Australian Council for Educational Research, 1990.

Exploring Mental Computation

Being able to calculate mentally, without the use of external memory aids (including paper and pencil) is a valuable skill. The illustrations demonstrate that doing computations mentally is often easier and quicker than performing written algorithms. One of the benefits of mental computation is that it can lead to a better understanding of place value, mathematical operations, and basic number properties. The cassette tape example $(2 \times \$3.99 = 2 \times \$4.00 - 2 \times 1¢)$ demonstrates mental application of the distributive property and involves both operations and basic number properties.

Research shows that students tend to rely on written computational algorithms and do not consider mental computation a viable option—perhaps because they have learned that in school, everything must be written. Students need encouragement to develop mental-computation skills and to apply them whenever they are appropriate.

Mental computation lends itself to a variety of thinking strategies. For example, consider these three approaches to calculating how much money 11 quarters is:

- 12×25 is $3.00, minus 25¢ is $2.75.

- 10×25 is $2.50, so 11×25 is 25¢ more or $2.75.

- 8×25 is $2.00, so 11×25 is three quarters or 75¢ more, so the total is $2.75.

As students learn to manipulate numbers in their heads, they develop better number sense and an increased confidence in their mathematical abilities. This confidence will encourage them to consider mental computation as an option when straightforward calculations are encountered. Regular opportunities to develop and apply mental computation not only contribute to number sense, but can significantly improve students' ability to think about numbers in a variety of ways.

Will You Do It in Your Head?

Number Sense Focus

- Mental computation
- Number relationships

Number Focus

- Activities 1–4: Whole numbers
- Activity 5: Fractions

Mathematical Background

Research shows that students often apply written algorithms to computations that would be more efficient to do mentally. This reliance on pencil and paper probably reflects the emphasis given to written computation in school. Calculators are a powerful computational tool, but wise use of them should be encouraged. We should not automatically use a calculator any more than we should automatically use written algorithms.

Using the Activities

These activities encourage students to think about doing computations mentally and to reflect on appropriate computational alternatives.

1. In each activity, reveal the illustration at the top. Ask students for other ways to do the computation, and talk about the strategies they suggest. Survey them about which method they prefer: would they do the calculation mentally, with pencil and paper, or with a calculator? Encourage them to explain their choice; the sharing of their explanations is the heart of these activities.

2. Show the computations one at a time, and ask students how they would prefer to do each one. Focus attention on the notion that the numbers and operations involved determine the mental computational difficulty. For example, 125 + 39 lends itself to mental computation. On the other hand, it would be difficult to calculate an exact answer for 125 ÷ 39 mentally, but easy to estimate if we think about 120 ÷ 40.

3. Make a list of the "easy" problems offered, which will reveal a range of computations and help students realize that what is easy for them may not be easy for everyone. Encourage students to explain why they find a particular computation easy.

Extending the Activities

- Ask students to make up a new computation that is easy to do mentally and to explain why it is easy.

- Ask for another computation that is hard to do mentally, and ask students to explain why it is hard.

Will You Do It in Your Head?

Which of these calculations are easy for you to do in your head? Why?

1. 8 + 5

2. 80 + 50

3. 8 + 50

4. 88 + 58

5. 888 + 58

6. 8 + 8 + 8 + 8 + 8

7. 88 + 88 + 88

8. 800 + 8 + 80

9. 18 + 17 + 16

10. 8 + 7 + 6

Will You Do It in Your Head?

Which of these calculations are easy for you to do in your head? Why?

1. 125 – 36

2. 26 – 15

3. 14 – 6

4. 83 – 27

5. 140 – 60

6. 130 – 27

7. 260 – 150

8. 260 – 15

9. 264 – 187

10. 8765 – 765

Will You Do It in Your Head?

Which of these calculations are easy for you to do in your head? Why?

1. 38×3

2. 4×9

3. 40×9

4. 63×24

5. 25×12

6. 136×2

7. 99×7

8. 5×26

9. 5×10

10. 10×53

Will You Do It in Your Head?

Which of these calculations are easy for you to do in your head? Why?

1. 20 ÷ 5

2. 630 ÷ 9

3. 42 ÷ 7

4. 500 ÷ 50

5. 360 ÷ 12

6. 870 ÷ 10

7. 593 ÷ 7

8. 48 ÷ 2

9. 350 ÷ 70

10. 240 ÷ 24

Will You Do It in Your Head?

Which of these calculations are easy for you to do in your head? Why?

1. $1 - \dfrac{1}{3}$

2. $\dfrac{1}{4} + \dfrac{1}{4} + \dfrac{1}{2}$

3. $1\dfrac{1}{4} - \dfrac{1}{2}$

4. $\dfrac{1}{4} + \dfrac{1}{8}$

5. $\dfrac{7}{8} - \dfrac{1}{2}$

6. $\dfrac{7}{8} + \dfrac{3}{8}$

7. $5 - 1\dfrac{1}{2}$

8. $\dfrac{2}{3} + \dfrac{2}{3} + \dfrac{2}{3}$

9. $2\dfrac{1}{4} - 1\dfrac{1}{4}$

10. $\dfrac{1}{3} + \dfrac{1}{2}$

EXPERIENCE 2

•••••••••••••••••••••••••••••

How Many Dots?

Number Sense Focus

• Mental computation

Number Focus

• Activities 1–3: Whole numbers

Mathematical Background

•••••••••••••••••••••••••••••

The abilities to see spatial relationships, to recognize and analyze patterns, and to use the resulting images to count and quantify are valuable number sense skills.

Using the Activities

•••••••••••••••••••••••••••••

In these activities, students are shown collection of dots for a short time. To mentally calculate how many dots are in each group, students must rely on arranging the dots they saw into recognizable patterns.

1. In Activity 1, show the first set of dots for several seconds. Cover the image, and invite students to say how many dots they think they saw. Emphasize that they should not simply guess the number of dots but find a strategy for mentally calculating the number. You may want students to work in pairs and share strategies. Show the image again if necessary. You may need to establish that each frame holds 10 dots when filled.

2. Ask individuals or pairs to share their answers and strategies. For example:

   • "I saw 5 rows of 2, which makes 10, and there were 2 of them, which makes 20."

   • "I saw 2 full cartons, which makes 20."

   • "I saw 4 groups of 5 each, so there are 20."

3. Use the remaining sets in Activity 1 in the same way. Discuss with students why the last diagram is more difficult. *(Because the dots do not form a pattern.)*

4. Use Activities 2 and 3 in the same way. In Activity 3, ask students how many squares do not have dots, and ask them to describe their strategy.

Extending the Activities

• •

• Ask students to make their own "10 frames" and challenge each other.

How Many Dots?

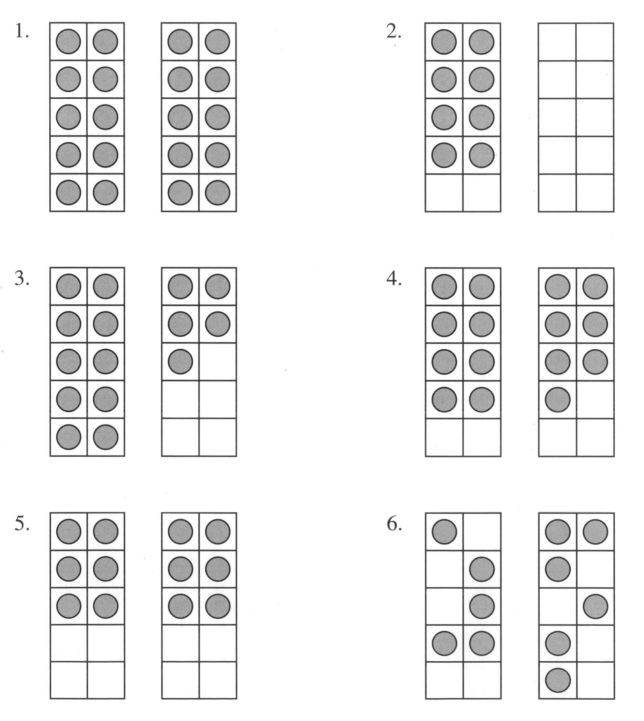

How many dots do you see? How did you count them?

Number SENSE / Grades 3–4

How Many Dots?

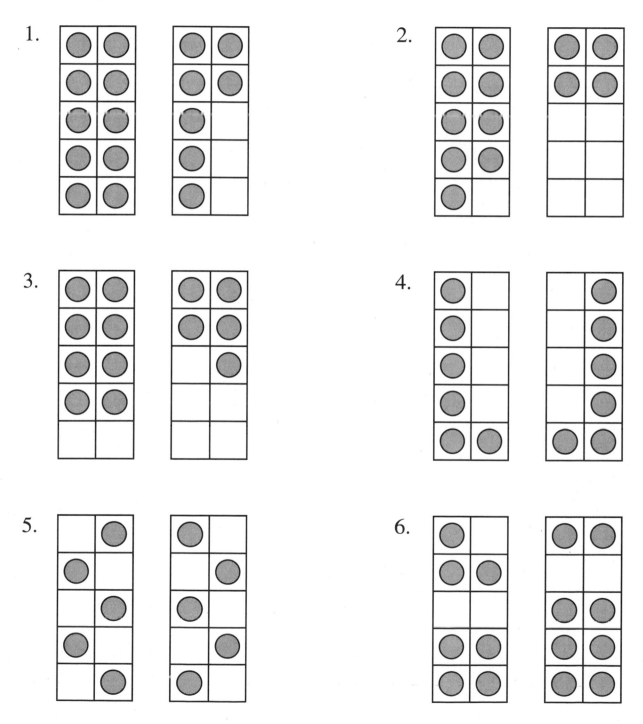

How many dots do you see? How did you count them?

How Many Dots?

1.

2.

3.

4.

How many dots do you see? How did you count them?

Today's Target

Number Sense Focus

- Mental computation
- Number relationships
- Multiple representation

Number Focus

- Activities 1–4. Whole numbers, fractions, decimals

Mathematical Background

We frequently use relationships between numbers to simplify mental calculations. To add 24 + 47, for example, we could use the relationship 47 = 50 − 3 and calculate 24 + 50 − 3. The ability to quickly see the relationships among numbers helps us to choose calculation strategies.

Using the Activities

In these activities, students are presented with a target number and are invited to create calculations for which the target number is the answer.

1. In each activity, reveal the target number. Ask for some calculations that would produce the number. You might make a list of several of the students' suggestions as a demonstration that numbers have multiple representations.

2. Reveal each restriction in turn, and ask for calculations of this type that produce the target number. Third-grade classes will not be able to use a decimal until the end of the year.

3. You or a student can suggest the target number for Activity 4. Numbers between 5 and 30 prompt a variety of suggestions from student.

Extending the Activities

- Invite students to challenge the class with a restriction of their own for a given target number.

- Create other restrictions and other target numbers, such as the date or the day of the year.

- Challenge the class to work individually to write as many calculations as possible that produce the target number in a given amount of time (say, 2 minutes). To encourage creativity, make a rule that a calculation will score only if no one else in class has thought of it.

Today's Target

Today's target is **8**

Try to make today's target in each of these ways.

1. Adding two numbers

2. Finding the difference of two numbers

3. Multiplying two numbers

4. Adding three numbers

5. Adding and subtracting

6. Multiplying and adding

7. Multiplying and subtracting

8. Using a fraction

9. Using a decimal

10. Doing it an unusual way

Today's Target

Today's target is **10**

Try to make today's target in each of these ways.

1. Adding two numbers

2. Finding the difference of two numbers

3. Multiplying two numbers

4. Adding three numbers

5. Adding and subtracting

6. Multiplying and adding

7. Multiplying and subtracting

8. Using a fraction

9. Using a decimal

10. Doing it an unusual way

Today's Target

Today's target is **15**

Try to make today's target in each of these ways.

1. Adding two numbers

2. Finding the difference of two numbers

3. Multiplying two numbers

4. Adding three numbers

5. Adding and subtracting

6. Multiplying and adding

7. Multiplying and subtracting

8. Using a fraction

9. Using a decimal

10. Doing it an unusual way

Today's Target

Today's target is ☐

Try to make today's target in each of these ways.

1. Adding two numbers

2. Finding the difference of two numbers

3. Multiplying two numbers

4. Adding three numbers

5. Adding and subtracting

6. Multiplying and adding

7. Multiplying and subtracting

8. Using a fraction

9. Using a decimal

10. Doing it an unusual way

Adding Compatibles

Number Sense Focus

- Mental computation
- Number relationships

Number Focus

- Activities 1–4: Whole numbers

Mathematical Background

Numbers that are easy to compute mentally and seem to go together naturally are called *compatible numbers*. For example, $16 + 84$ and $\frac{1}{4} + \frac{3}{4}$ are compatible numbers for addition; 25×4 are compatible numbers for multiplication. Compatible numbers help simplify mental computations. To solve $34 + 8$, we may reason that $34 + 6 = 40$, and 2 more makes 42. To add $4 + 3 + 8 + 7 + 6$, we may reason that $4 + 6 = 10$, and $3 + 7 = 10$, and $20 + 8 = 28$.

Using the Activities

In these activities, students are shown a grid of numbers and are challenged to find sets of two or more cells in a row (horizontally or vertically) with a given sum.

1. You may want to provide paper copies of the activities to small groups of students. Invite students to circle sets of numbers that add to the given sum. Remind them that they can use each number in only one combination.

2. Activity 4 challenges students to find compatible pairs of numbers for doing chain addition.

Solutions

Activity 1

4	6	1	6	3	8
3	7	6	5	2	2
5	4	2	5	4	1
2	6	2	3	4	9
3	8	2	6	8	2
2	1	7	1	4	6

Activity 2

3	17	8	5	15	7
11	0	12	2	9	13
9	20	1	18	11	6
8	7	19	17	3	14
12	13	20	5	7	13
6	14	0	15	10	10

Activity 3

43	7	16	25	25	16
23	20	34	42	19	34
27	30	21	8	31	11
18	50	29	37	13	39
32	0	47	15	17	40
10	40	3	35	33	10

Activity 4

Row sums: 100, 50, 300, 250, 300, 300. Total sum: 1300.

Extending the Activities

• •

- Have students create their own grids for compatible numbers and exchange their games with others to solve.

Adding Compatibles

4	6	1	6	3	8
3	7	6	5	2	2
5	4	2	5	4	1
2	6	2	3	4	9
3	8	2	6	8	2
2	1	7	1	4	6

Find two or more numbers in a row—across or down—with a sum of 10.

Adding Compatibles

3	17	8	5	15	7
11	0	12	2	9	13
9	20	1	18	11	6
8	7	19	17	3	14
12	13	20	5	7	13
6	14	0	15	10	10

Find two or more numbers in a row—across or down—with a sum of 20.

Adding Compatibles

43	7	16	25	25	16
23	20	34	42	19	34
27	30	21	8	31	11
18	50	29	37	13	39
32	0	47	15	17	40
10	40	3	35	33	10

Find two or more numbers in a row—across or down—with a sum of 50.

Adding Compatibles

Row
sums

18	25	12	14	25	6	_____
6	7	14	13	5	5	_____
7	19	81	93	49	51	_____
25	67	33	75	32	18	_____
88	23	12	77	91	9	_____
19	52	48	81	35	65	_____

Total sum _____

Find the sum of each row of numbers.

What is the total of all the numbers?

Which Path Will You Take?

Number Sense Focus

- Mental computation
- Multiple representation

Number Focus

- Activities 1 5: Whole numbers

Mathematical Background

Mental computation helps us to think about numbers, to recognize numbers that are easy to compute, to apply mathematical properties, and to explore relationships. For example, we could compute $5 + 10 - 10$ by thinking that 5 plus 10 is 15, and 15 minus 10 is 5. A more efficient solution would take advantage of the fact that $10 - 10$ is 0.

Using the Activities

In these activities, students practice mental computation in an interesting and challenging context. You may want to distribute paper copies of the mazes so students can record their thinking.

1. In Activities 1, 2, and 3, make sure students understand that they begin at the bottom with the Start Number and travel along the various people's paths by performing the computations shown.

2. The blank mazes in Activities 4 and 5 may be used in several ways:

   - Ask students to write in the values and operations and then compute each person's number.

   - Provide numbers for each person, and have students enter appropriate values and operations.

   - Provide all the numbers, and have students enter operations that will produce the correct results.

Solutions

Activity 1

1. Alex
2. Ellen
3. Dante, 45
4. Batai and Cole, 10.
5. Flora, 65.

Activity 2

1. Aaron and Colin
2. Frannie's
3. 30
4. Elke, 50.
5. The Start Number would have to be 5. Aaron's number would remain the same because 0 is still a factor.

Activity 3

1. Ami, Barb, and Joan
2. Ira and Marque
3. Drew and Errol
4. Kendra
5. Fanny

Extending the Activities

• •

- Ask students to change the Start Number and observe how the people's numbers change.

- Ask students to change one operation at a particular step and find the new results.

- Challenge students to create their own mazes that produce certain results.

Which Path Will You Take?

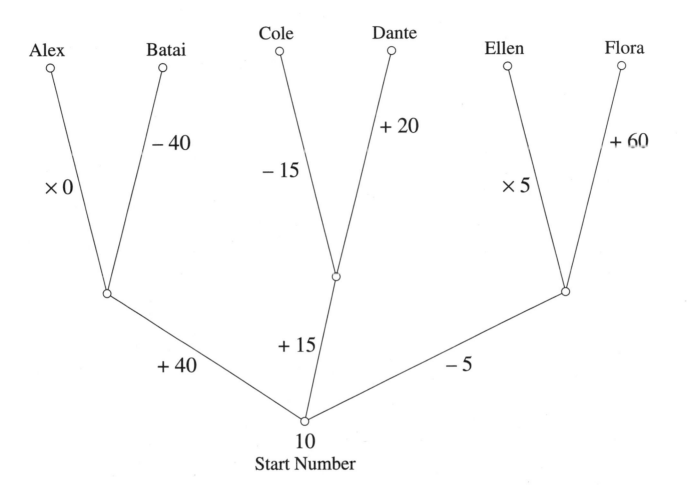

1. Whose path gives 0?

2. Whose path gives 25?

3. What does Dante's path give?

4. Which two paths give the same number?

5. Whose path gives the largest number?

Which Path Will You Take?

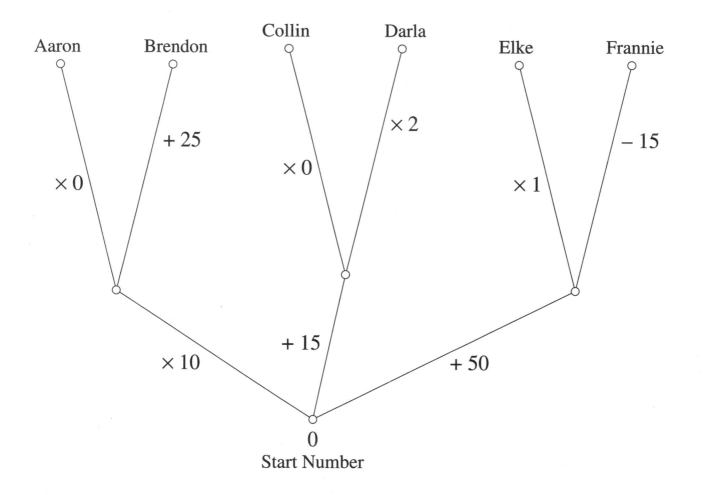

1. Whose path gives 0?

2. Whose path gives 35?

3. What does Darla's path give?

4. Whose path gives the largest number?

5. What would the Start Number have to be for Brendon's path to give 75? Would Aaron's number change?

Which Path Will You Take?

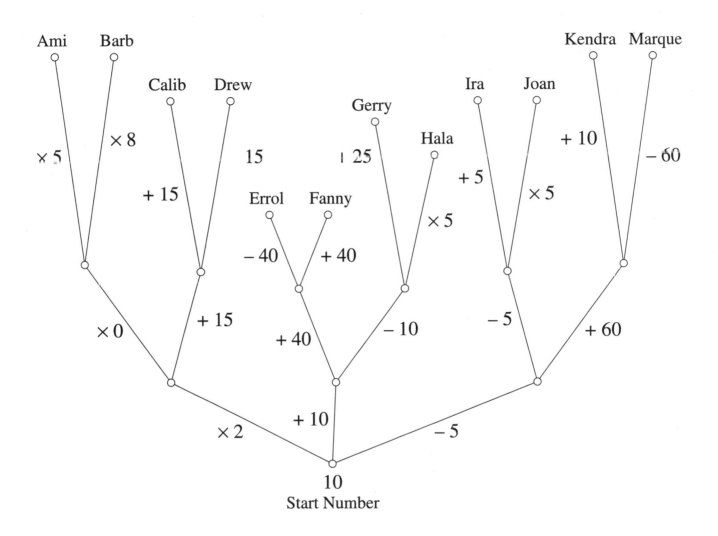

Whose path gives

1. 0?   2. 5?   3. 20?   4. 75?   5. 100?

Which Path Will You Take?

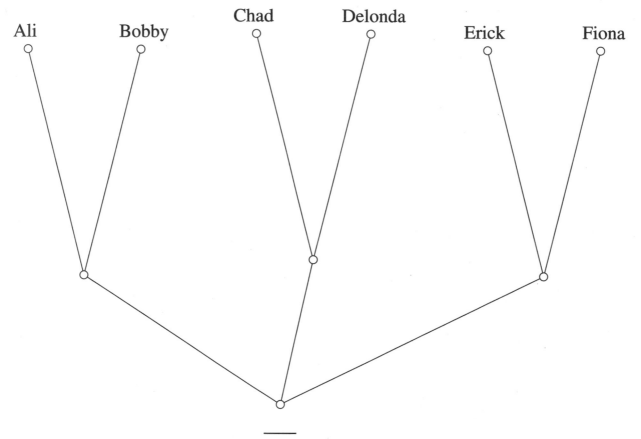

Ali   Bobby   Chad   Delonda   Erick   Fiona

Start Number

Write numbers and operations to make your own paths.

What does each path give?

Which Path Will You Take?

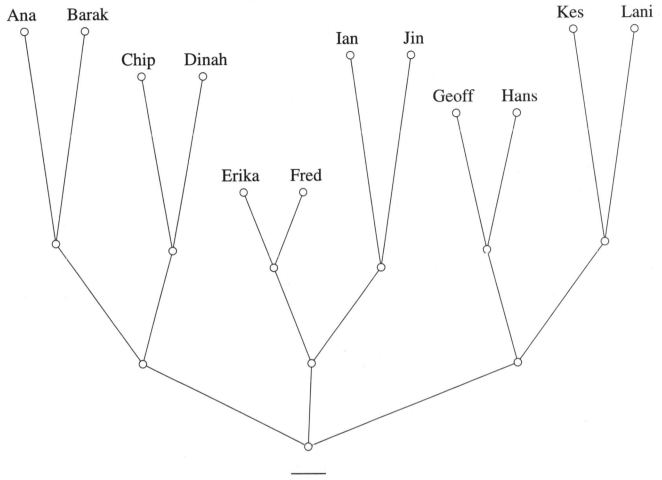

Start Number

Write numbers and operations to make your own paths.

What does each path give?

EXPERIENCE 6

Sorting Answers

Number Sense Focus

- Mental computation
- Relative size

Number Focus

- Activities 1–3: Whole numbers

Mathematical Background

The ability to mentally compute sums, differences, and products develops with regular opportunities to do such computation. And, once students find an answer, it is important that they think about the relative size of the answer.

Using the Activities

These activities combine mental computation with the ordering of numbers by their relative size.

1. As a warm-up, copy this illustration onto the board:

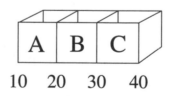

Explain that the drawing shows how numbers can be sorted into each box—for example, numbers between 20 and 30 can be put into Box B. Ask students to name several numbers that belong in each box. What is the largest number that can be placed in Box B? What is the smallest number? These questions address what to do with values falling on a boundary, such as 30. Different answers can be defended; the important issue is to decide on a consistent plan for handling boundary values.

2. Either make a copy of each activity for the students, or ask them to draw lines on a piece of paper (such as __ __ __ __ __ __ __), where the number of lines is equal to the number of boxes shown.

3. In each activity, ask students to decide which sum, difference, or product goes where and to write the correct letter in the boxes. Have them describe how they solved the problems. Encourage a variety of explanations.

Solutions

Activity 1

1. MONKEYS
2. BADGERS

Activity 2

1. TRIANGLE
2. PENTAGON

Activity 3

1. DOUGHNUT
2. FISHCAKE

Extending the Activities

• •

- Ask students to propose other computations that belong in a particular box.

- Ask students to make up computation problems that have results between certain values—such as 10 to 90, 5 to 55, or 50 to 120—and explain how they constructed their problems.

- Invite students to construct a series of mental computations that will reveal a secret message.

Sorting Answers

1. Put each letter in the correct box.

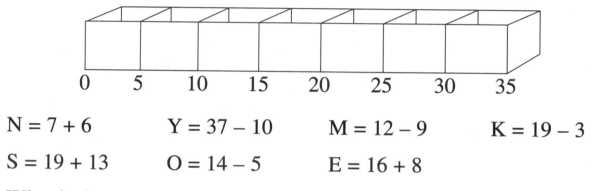

0   5   10   15   20   25   30   35

$N = 7 + 6$ $Y = 37 - 10$ $M = 12 - 9$ $K = 19 - 3$

$S = 19 + 13$ $O = 14 - 5$ $E = 16 + 8$

What is the secret word?

2. Put each letter in the correct box.

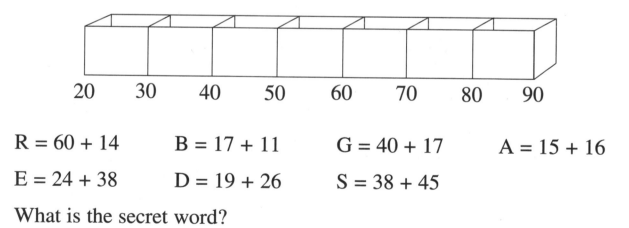

20   30   40   50   60   70   80   90

$R = 60 + 14$ $B = 17 + 11$ $G = 40 + 17$ $A = 15 + 16$

$E = 24 + 38$ $D = 19 + 26$ $S = 38 + 45$

What is the secret word?

Sorting Answers

1. Put each letter in the correct box.

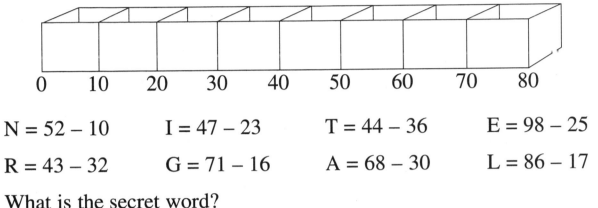

N = 52 – 10   I = 47 – 23   T = 44 – 36   E = 98 – 25

R = 43 – 32   G = 71 – 16   A = 68 – 30   L = 86 – 17

What is the secret word?

2. Put each letter in the correct box.

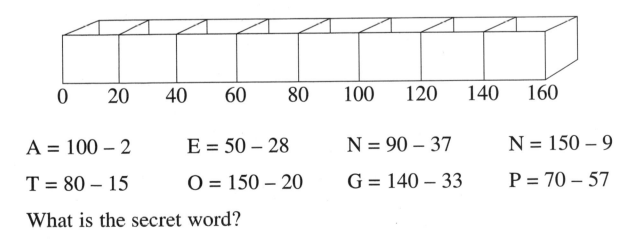

A = 100 – 2   E = 50 – 28   N = 90 – 37   N = 150 – 9

T = 80 – 15   O = 150 – 20   G = 140 – 33   P = 70 – 57

What is the secret word?

Sorting Answers

1. Put each letter in the correct box.

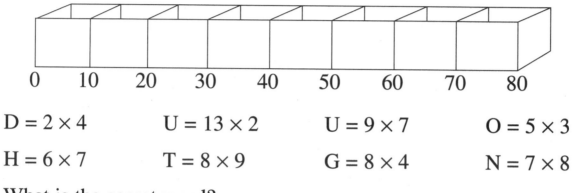

| 0 | 10 | 20 | 30 | 40 | 50 | 60 | 70 | 80 |

$D = 2 \times 4$ $U = 13 \times 2$ $U = 9 \times 7$ $O = 5 \times 3$

$H = 6 \times 7$ $T = 8 \times 9$ $G = 8 \times 4$ $N = 7 \times 8$

What is the secret word?

2. Put each letter in the correct box.

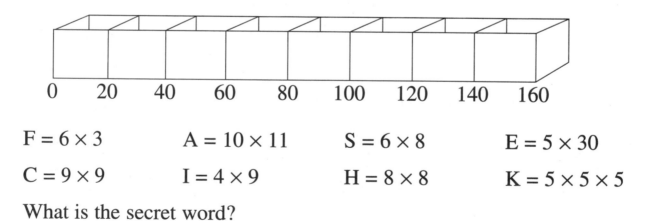

| 0 | 20 | 40 | 60 | 80 | 100 | 120 | 140 | 160 |

$F = 6 \times 3$ $A = 10 \times 11$ $S = 6 \times 8$ $E = 5 \times 30$

$C = 9 \times 9$ $I = 4 \times 9$ $H = 8 \times 8$ $K = 5 \times 5 \times 5$

What is the secret word?

....

Postage Stamp Math

Number Sense Focus

- Mental computation
- Number relationships

Number Focus

- Activities 1–3: Whole numbers

Mathematical Background

••••••••••••••••••••••••••••

Postage stamps are designed in a wide range of sizes, styles, and values, and we must examine them carefully when we use them. Sheets of stamps are natural array models for skip counting and multiplication, and they promote number recognition and mental computation.

Using the Activities

••••••••••••••••••••••••••••

1. Find out what your students already know about stamps. Are all stamps the same size? Are they all the same value? What are some different values of stamps? Examine some real stamps. Are the values shown? (Stamps in the United States typically show a numeral but no ¢ or $ sign; the unit is assumed to be known from the context.) If any students collect stamps, ask them to share some ways stamps can be classified.

2. In Activity 1, show the collection of stamps, and ask these questions:

   - Find two stamps with the same value. Find two that are the same size. Do all stamps of the same size also have the same value?

   - Order the stamps from the smallest value to the largest value.

   - Which stamps could you buy with a dime? with a quarter? for exactly 50¢?

- Identify two stamps you could buy with $1. What change would you receive?

- Estimate the total value of all the stamps. *($3.25)*

3. In Activity 2, ask students these questions:

- Which stamp is worth the most? the least?

- Which stamps could you buy with a dime? with a quarter?

- If you bought stamps for 70¢ and received a penny in change, which stamps did you buy?

- Which pairs of stamps are worth exactly 50¢?

- List all the different amounts of money you could spend in buying two of these stamps.

- Estimate the total value of all the stamps. *($2.86)*

4. The array of stamps in Activity 3 lends itself to several activities.

- Show the array for several seconds. Cover the image, and ask students to estimate the number of stamps that were shown. Have them share how they made their estimates.

- Use the array to encourage skip counting. Mask a number of columns, and then reveal rows one at a time. Ask students to count out loud as each row is revealed. For example, mask off five columns. Reveal the first row and say "5," reveal the second row and say "10," and so on.

- Do array multiplication as a class. For example, mask stamps to show a 4 by 6 array, and ask students how many stamps are showing.

- Connect any of the above activities to money. For example, when skip counting, you might say "5 cents," "10 cents," and so on, and write several of their representations as they are said aloud. Five cents might be written as 5¢, $0.05, or 5 cents.

Extending the Activities

- -

- Ask students to call or visit a post office to research what stamp values can be bought and the number of stamps on a sheet for a particular stamp, and then determine the value of each sheet.

Postage Stamp Math

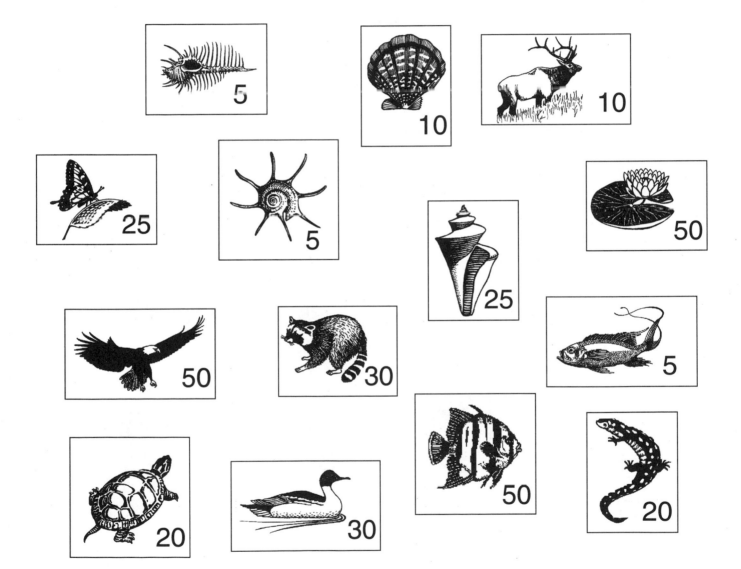

Postage Stamp Math

Postage Stamp Math

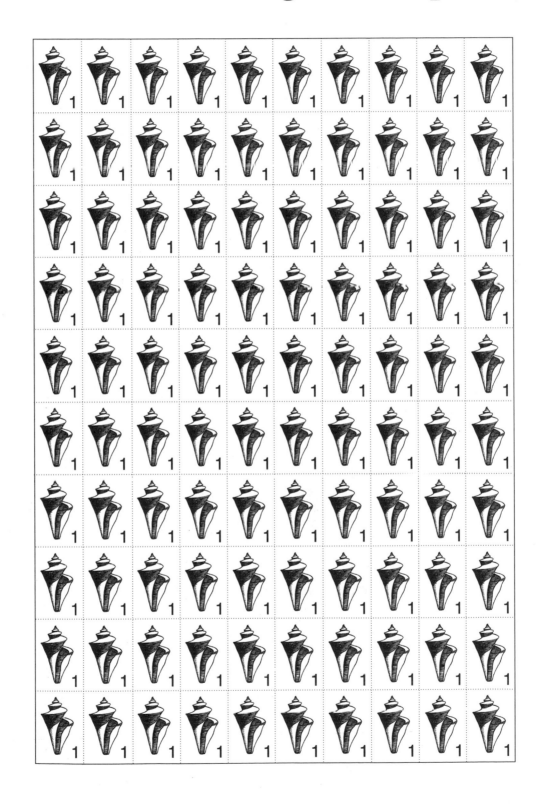

EXPERIENCE 8

....

Different Dollars

Number Sense Focus

- Mental computation
- Multiple representation

Number Focus

- Activities 1–3: Whole numbers, decimals

Mathematical Background

....

Money naturally lends itself to mental computation because denominations are generally related to 10. Countries around the world have different currency systems, but several—for example, Australia, Canada, and the United States—use dollars. The dollars look different and have varying buying power. Experiences with different dollars provide a multicultural connection and encourage students to think about relationships between currency systems.

Using the Activities

....

1. In Activity 1, ask students the value of each coin shown and to find the coin worth most and the one worth least. Ask these questions such as these:

   - Which group of coins contains the greatest amount of money? Which contains the least amount of money?

   - If you cover any three coins, what is the greatest amount of money you can cover? What is the least amount of money you can cover?

   - What equivalent relationships do you see? (Offer an example of an equivalent relationship, such as that a dime is equivalent to two nickels, or two quarters make a half dollar.)

   - What is the total amount of money shown? First estimate the answer, then calculate it. *($2.10)*

2. As a warm-up for Activity 2 or 3, ask whether anyone has traveled to another country and, if so, whether they have any foreign currency to show or tell about. Ask questions similar to those you asked in Activity 1.

3. After Activity 2 or 3, ask questions to encourage students to talk about differences and similarities in the monetary systems of Australia, Canada, and the United States. Help them understand that although all three countries use dollars and cents, and all have a 10¢ coin, they have *different* coins. For example, Australia has no 1¢ or 25¢ coin, and the Canadian and Australian dollars are coins rather than bills.

Extending the Activities

• Point out that Australia has no pennies. Talk about what would happen if pennies were no longer minted in the United States.

• Ask students to find out which is worth more based on today's exchange rate: a Canadian dollar or a United States dollar. How about a Canadian dollar and an Australian dollar? How about a United States dollar and an Australian dollar?

Different Dollars

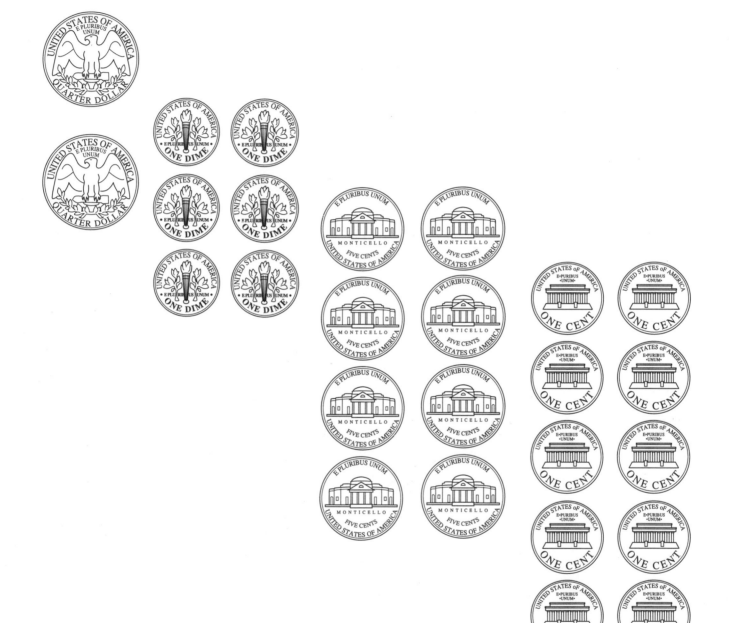

What country uses this money?

Number SENSE / Grades 3–4

Different Dollars

What country uses this money?

Different Dollars

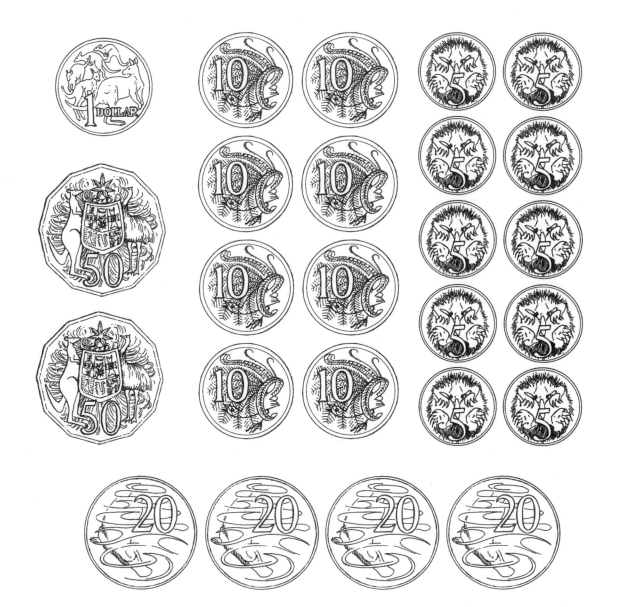

What country uses this money?

Number SENSE / Grades 3–4

Exploring Multiple Representation

24 is the number of
hours in a day.

24 is 1 less than 25

$$25 - 1 = 24$$

24 is the number of
cans of soda in a case.

24 is two
dozen eggs.

24 is 2 dimes
and 4 pennies.

Numbers may be expressed using a variety of symbolic and graphical representations. For example:

- $\frac{3}{4}$ is equivalent to $\frac{6}{8}$, 0.75, and three out of four.

- 30 cents is 3 dimes or a quarter plus a nickel.

- Two hours is 120 minutes.

- The number 8 may be expressed by the word *eight*, the symbol 8, or a drawing: ◯ ◯ ◯ ◯ ◯ ◯ ◯ ◯

- The expression $2 + 2 + 2 + 2$ is the same as 4×2.

Understanding multiple representation, recognizing that some representations are more useful than others in certain problem-solving situations, and being able to generate equivalent representations are essential number sense skills.

For example, suppose a person checking out at a market has a bill of $8.53. The person could pay with a $10 bill and get $1.47 change. However, if the customer wanted to carry fewer coins, he or she could pay with a $10 bill and 3 pennies, and receive change of $1.50. The rationale is based on decomposing $8.53 into $8.50 + $0.03.

Activities in this section promote several ways to think about equivalent forms of numbers. Students need experiences in thoughtfully breaking numbers apart—decomposing—and putting them together—recomposing—in different but equivalent ways. The ability to recognize and create numerical representations that simplify problems is an indication of high-level mathematical thinking.

Every Picture Suggests a Story

Number Sense Focus

- Multiple representation

Number Focus

- Activities 1–3: Whole numbers

Mathematical Background

The ability to make sense of quantitative data presented in pictorial or graphical form is an important number sense skill. Students need to feel comfortable inferring information from the shape of the line, the relative size of the columns, and the pattern of the data points in graphical displays.

Using the Activities

In these activities, students are presented with visual information and asked to invent situations that the pictures or graphs might describe. The emphasis is on realistically interpreting the quantitative information.

1. Show the first graph in Activity 1. Explain that the graph is showing some information but, because no title or labels are given, we cannot tell what the graph is about.

2. Invite students to invent a story to go with the graph. Emphasize that the story should contain numbers that fit the picture. Here are two explanations students have created for this graph:

   - "The graph is about the number of people in our families. There are six in mine, three in Renee's, and four in Ana's."

   - "The graph shows how much money we have saved. I have $6, Martina has $3, and Darnell has $4."

3. Show each of the other pictures, and ask for stories to fit them. Encourage discussion about the extent to which each story offered fits the visual information and is realistic.

4. Conduct Activities 2 and 3 in the same way. In Activity 3, students will encounter the same data displayed in different ways. Show two pictures at a time, and encourage students to tell a story or to describe why the days (or months) are grouped as they are. They may recognize other possibilities, but here are two suggestions: In part 1, the days of the week are grouped by their first letter and then by weekdays and weekend days. In part 2, the months of the year are grouped by season and then according to the number of letters they contain.

Solutions

Stories will vary; one scenario is presented for each picture in Activities 1 and 2.

Activity 1

1. On the first day of the fair I competed in 6 events, on the second 3 events, and on the third I entered 4.
2. My two sisters and I each bought four books at the school sale.
3. Two weeks ago I made $10, last week I made $5, and this week I made $12.
4. My older brother gave me his change every day this week. On Monday he gave me 70¢, on Tuesday 90¢, on Wednesday 25¢, on Thursday 50¢, and on Friday $1.00.

Activity 2

1. Our club has five members. Three of us—Bakari, Susan, and Jose— each have a pet cat; Mali and Roman don't have a cat.
2. I grouped together all the shapes that had their sides equal and angles equal.
3. Every month one more person joined our club. This shows our club's membership over the first five months.
4. Each month we collected more money toward our club's goal of $1000. By the end of the first month, we had made about $200, and in the five months, we reached our goal.

Extending the Activities
• •

- Ask students to create their own graphs and stories to accompany them.

- Challenge students to collect examples of graphs from newspapers and magazines and write about them.

Every Picture Suggests a Story

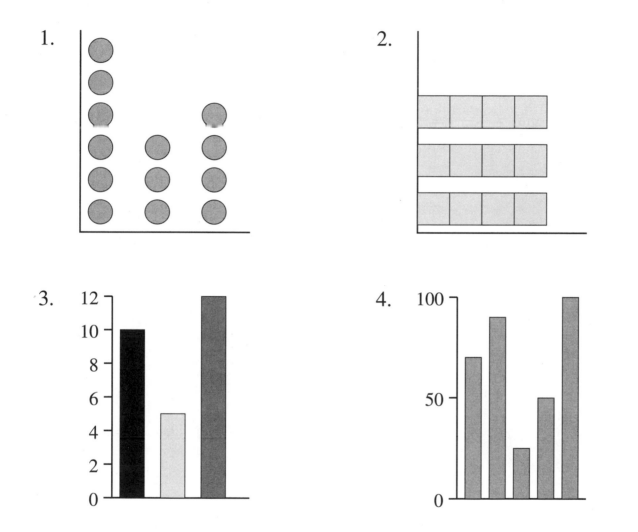

Make up a story to fit each picture.

Every Picture Suggests a Story

1.
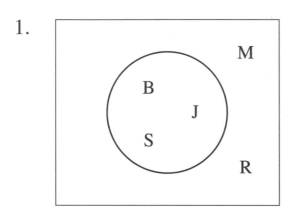

2.
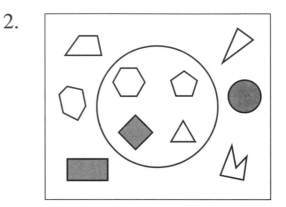

3.
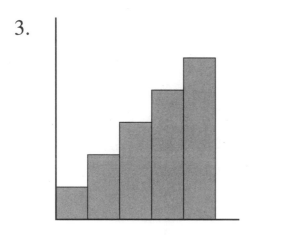

4.
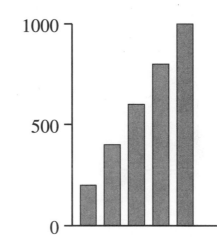

Make up a story to fit each picture.

Number SENSE / Grades 3–4

Every Picture Suggests a Story

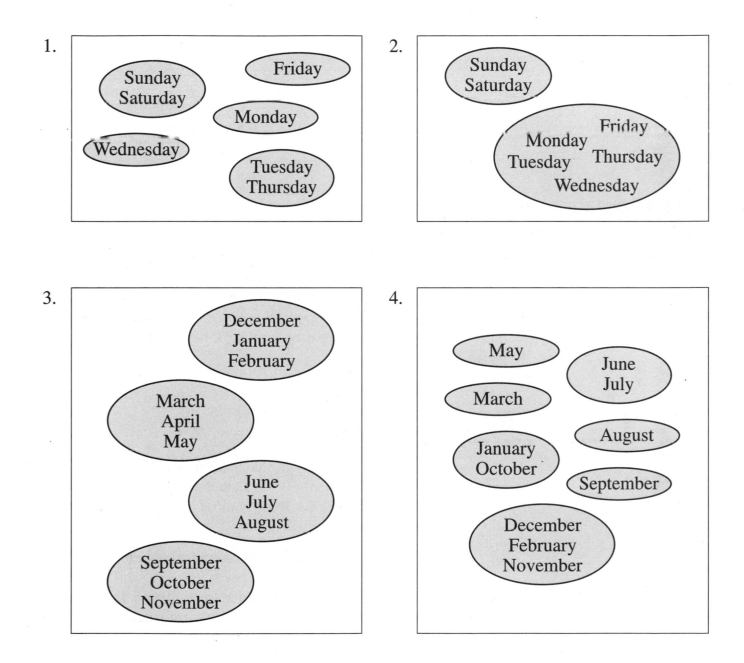

Make up a story to fit each picture.

• •

Making Number Chains

Number Sense Focus

- Multiple representation
- Mental computation

Number Focus

- Activity 1: Whole numbers

Mathematical Background

• •

Counting and ordering numbers are important early steps in developing number sense. These kinesthetic games encourage students to order numbers in different ways. Students will gain a perspective of multiple representation as they realize, for example, that two more for one person is the same as two fewer for another person, or that 70 is 20 more than 50 but 20 less than 90.

Using the Activity

• •

1. To prepare for these games, assign students numbers that are multiples of 10 starting from 10. Then, ask each student to design and color a number crown that displays his or her number from the front and back large enough so everyone can see it.

2. As a warm-up, have one student call out a number between 50 and 300. Ask a second student to tell what number is 10 more than the named number, and a third student to tell what number is 10 less. For example, if the first student calls out 230, the second student would say 240 and the third 220.

3. Reveal the rules for the first game, or simply review the rules yourself and describe them to the class. Let students walk about the room to find the number 10 higher and 10 lower than their number and join hands to form a chain. Once the chain is complete, explore questions such as these:

- Is everyone holding hands with two different people? *(no)* Who isn't? *(the ends of the chain)*

- How does your number compare to the number of the person on your left? *(10 more, except at the end of the chain.)*

- How does your number compare to the number of the second person on right? *(20 less, except at the end of the chain.)*

4. Games 2 and 3 promote further exploration of patterns and relationships.

5. Talk about the results of each game as a class. For example, in Activity 2, two lines are formed, one following the sequence 10, 30, 50 and one the sequence 20, 40, 60. In Activity 3, not everyone will find a double, which raises interesting questions:

- Who did not find a double? Why?

- For those without a double, what would your double be?

- Is anyone's double an odd number? Why or why not?

Extending the Activity

- Ask students what would happen if everyone were looking for the number 40 (or 50 or 60) more than their number.

- Allow students to make up other rules and play Making Number Chains with each new rule. They might change the numbers they count off by as well.

- If your students are ready for a fraction version of the game, have them count off by $\frac{1}{2}$ and play Making Number Chains with new rules.

Making Number Chains

Game 1

Find the person who is 10 more than you. Take hold of that person's right hand with your left hand.

Game 2

Use 20 more than you.

Game 3

Use double your number.

....

Calculating Differently

Number Sense Focus

- Multiple representation
- Mental computation

Number Focus

- Activity 1: Whole numbers

Mathematical Background

•••••••••••••••••••••••••••

Exploring different ways to represent numbers stimulates creative thinking and offers practice with basic facts and the application of operations and important number relationships. This activity may also initiate a discussion about the order of operations.

Using the Activity

•••••••••••••••••••••••••••

Every student or pair of students will need a four-function calculator for this activity.

1. Indicate the 8 in the calculator display. Explain that the goal is to start with 8 and end with 16 without clearing the calculator. If you have an overhead calculator, start with an 8 in the display. Ask students what operations they could perform to move from 8 to 16. For example:

$$8 + 8 = 16 \qquad 8 \times 4 \div 2 = 16 \qquad 8 + 2 + 2 + 2 + 2 = 16 \qquad 8 \times 2 = 16$$

2. Ask students to list the ways they find to get to 16 from 8. Remind them to record the keystrokes and operations they use.

3. As students work, you might ask them to copy their solutions onto the board, first making sure no other student has already listed that method. This will create a class list of methods that everyone can see and discuss.

4. Part 2 asks how students can get to 40 from 8. For example:

$$8 \times 5 = 40 \qquad\qquad 8 \times 10 - 40 = 40$$
$$8 \times 4 + 8 = 40 \qquad\qquad 8 + 12 + 20 = 40$$
$$8 \div 2 \times 10 = 40 \qquad\qquad 8 \times 50 \div 10 = 40$$
$$8 + 32 = 40 \qquad\qquad 8 + 8 + 8 + 8 + 8 = 40$$

Extending the Activity

• Present other beginning and ending numbers using the calculator at the bottom of the activity sheet.

• Present other beginning and ending numbers, and require that certain other numbers be used. For example: Go from 25 to 50, and use a 10 at least once. (Thus, $25 \times 2 = 50$ is not a legitimate solution; $25 + 10 + 15 = 50$ and $25 \times 10 - 200 = 50$ are.)

Calculating Differently

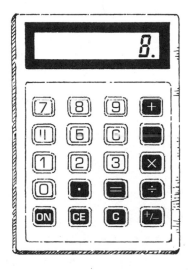

1. How can you start with 8 on your calculator and get 16?

2. How can you start with 8 on your calculator and get 40?

3. Use your calculator to try other numbers.

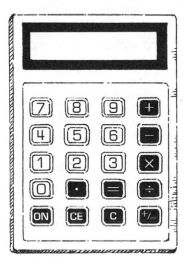

EXPERIENCE 12

••••••••••••••••••••••••••

How Could It Happen?

Number Sense Focus

- Multiple representation
- Mental computation

Number Focus

- Activities 1–4: Whole numbers

Mathematical Background

••••••••••••••••••••••••••••••••

These activities offer students opportunities to construct and generate equivalent relationships.

Using the Activities

••••••••••••••••••••••••••••••••

1. As a warm-up, ask students for different ways to make 10—such as 5×2, $12 - 2$, $6 + 4$, and $\frac{1}{2}$ of 20. Create a list of their suggestions.

2. In Activity 1, make sure students understand the rule for combining numbers. For each question, list the solutions that are proposed and discuss how each was found. You may want to have students search for all the possible answers to each question.

3. You might ask students to pretend that the circles are spinners. What number would they expect to come up most often on each spinner? What sum would come up most often? What product?

4. In Activities 2 and 3, continue to encourage students to explain their thinking as they answer the questions. Subtraction is allowed in Activity 2. Make it clear that the numbers can be used from the circles in either order as long as a smaller number is subtracted from a larger number.

5. Activity 4 allows students to create their own games. You might want to distribute paper copies to small groups and allow them to fill in the circles with numbers to give the desired results. They may want to experiment with numbers on small scraps of paper before filling in the circles. Have groups share their solutions.

Solutions

Activity 1

1. 1 and 5, 2 and 3, or 1 and 6
2. 8 and 6
3. 8 and 6
4. No, because $1 + 2$ is greater than 1×2.
5. 2, 3, 4, 5, 6, 7, 8, 9, 10, 11, 12, 13, 14, 15, 16, 18, 28, 32, 35, 40, 42, 48

Activity 2

1. Possible answers: $24 - 12$, $3 + 9$, 6×2; There are 14 ways to make 12.
2. There are 7 ways to make 20.
3. No, $16 - 15$ is one way to make 1.
4. Answers will vary.
5. Answers will vary, but 49 is the largest.

Activity 3

1. 4×5, 2×10
2. 200 and 0
3. 17 different results: 0, 1, 2, 3, 4, 5, 10, 15, 20, 25, 30, 40, 50, 75, 100, 150, 200
4. The spinner on the left could represent a penny, nickel, dime, quarter, and half dollar.
5. Stories will vary.

Activity 4

1. Answers will vary, but placing 0, 4, 8, and 12 on one spinner and 1, 2, 3, and 4 on the other will produce the numbers 1 to 16.
2. Answers will vary.

Extending the Activities

• •

- Add division as an operation, and have students explore the implications for each question.

- Have students place multiples of 10 on one circle and multiples of 100 on the other. Explore ways that these numbers can be added, subtracted, and multiplied.

- Suggest that students make up mysteries to go with each game. For example, in Activity 1, Barbara chose two numbers and got 28 by multiplying them and 11 by adding them. What could her numbers be?

How Could It Happen?

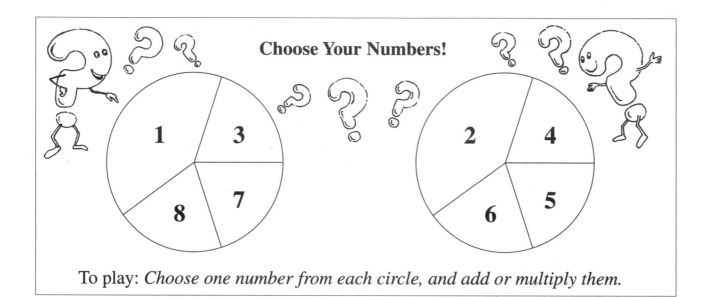

Choose Your Numbers!

To play: *Choose one number from each circle, and add or multiply them.*

1. Kara chose two numbers and got 6. What number did she pick from each circle?

2. Alistair got the largest sum possible.
    What numbers did he choose?

3. Masako got the largest product possible.
    What numbers did she choose?

4. Aaron says the smallest sum for this game
    is smaller than the smallest product. Is he right?

5. List all the possible results in this game.

How Could It Happen?

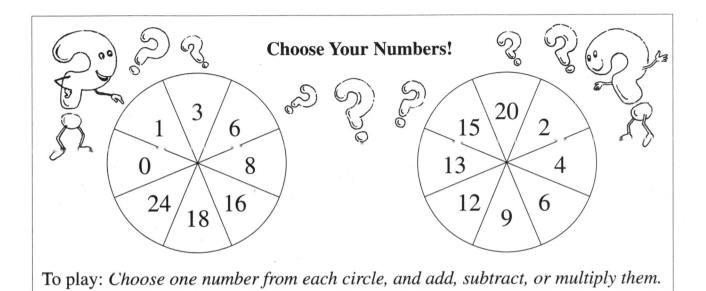

Choose Your Numbers!

To play: *Choose one number from each circle, and add, subtract, or multiply them.*

1. Alex chose two numbers and got 12. What could he have chosen? How many ways can you make 12 in this game?

2. Ty can make 20 in two ways. Daran can make 20 in three ways. How many ways can you make 20?

3. Sara says it is impossible to make 1. Is this true? How do you know?

4. List five different results you can get in this game.

5. Name a number under 50 that you can't get in this game.

How Could It Happen?

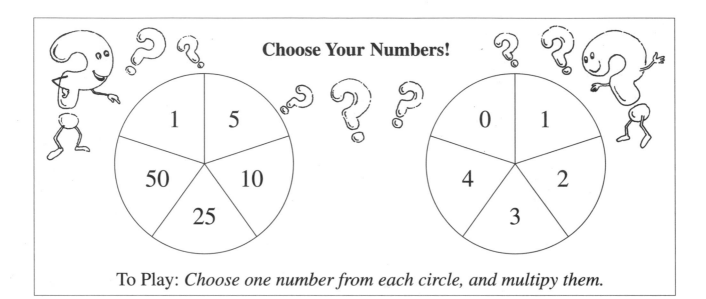

Choose Your Numbers!

To Play: *Choose one number from each circle, and multipy them.*

1. How could you make 20 in this game?

2. What are the highest and lowest results you can make?

3. How many different results can you get?

4. Suppose one circle represents coins. Which circle is it? Why?

5. Choose a number from each circle, and write a story that involves the numbers you chose.

How Could It Happen?

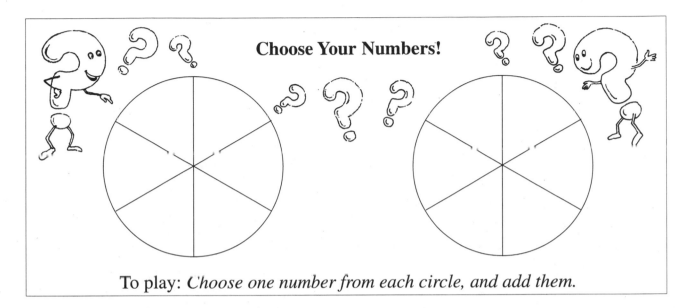

Choose Your Numbers!

To play: *Choose one number from each circle, and add them.*

1. Put numbers on each circle so that you can make the results 1, 2, 3, and so on, going as high as possible. How high can you go?

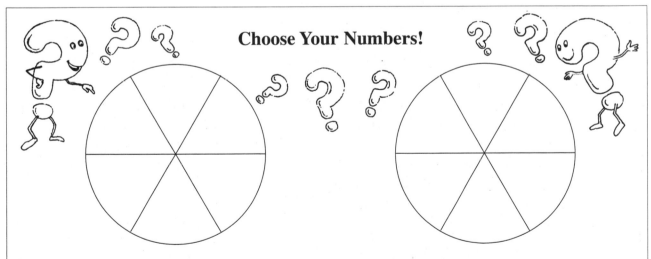

Choose Your Numbers!

To play: *Choose one number from each circle, and add, subtract, or multiply them.*

2. Put numbers on each circle so that you can make 1 and 100 in several different ways. List 5 other numbers you can make.

EXPERIENCE 13

How Did You Find Them?

Number Sense Focus

- Multiple representation
- Mental computation

Number Focus

- Activities 1–2: Whole numbers
- Activity 3: Decimals

Mathematical Background.

Part of good number sense is the ability to recognize different number combinations that produce the same result. It is also important to be familiar with *compatible numbers* (numbers that are easy to compute mentally and seem to go together naturally, such as $35 + 65$).

Using the Activities

These activities will encourage students to look for relationships among numbers and to recognize compatible numbers.

1. As a warm-up, give students a number less than 100, say 85. Ask: What number could be added to my number to get 90? Added to get more than 100? Subtracted to get a result less than 50? Subtracted to get a difference of 5? Added to get more than 100? You may need to talk about the word *difference* and its connection to subtraction.

2. In Activity 1, give students an opportunity to examine the values in the box, then explore the challenges one at a time. Be sure students realize that several correct answers may exist, and encourage them to share their thinking once they have found a solution. You can ask additional questions (Find a pair with a sum between 90 and 100, . . .) or students can ask questions for others to answer.

3. Activities 2 and 3 have parallel structures. Encourage students to make connections between the strategies they used with whole numbers in Activity 2 and with decimals in Activity 3.

Extending the Activities

• •

- Ask one student to name a number between 0 and 50. Have another student state a condition, such as, "A number that, added to the first number, gives more than 80." Make a list of correct answers as students call them out. Change numbers, operations, and range of acceptable responses as appropriate for your students.

How Did You Find Them?

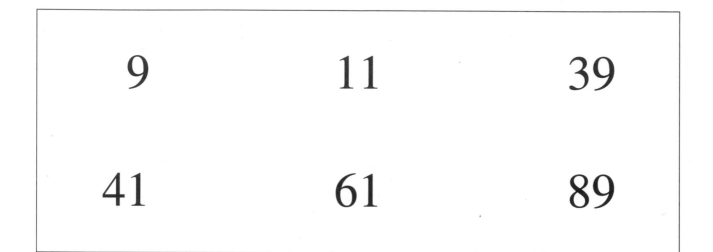

9	11	39
41	61	89

Pick a pair of numbers from the box . . .

1. with a sum less than 50.

2. so that when you subtract them you get 30.

3. with a difference of 50.

4. with a sum of 100.

5. with a sum more than 100.

Remember to tell how you found your pair.

How Did You Find Them?

50	150	350
450	650	850

Pick a pair of numbers . . .

1. with a difference of 100.

2. with a difference of 300.

3. with a sum of 500.

4. with a sum less than 500.

5. with a sum more than 1000.

Remember to tell how you found your pair.

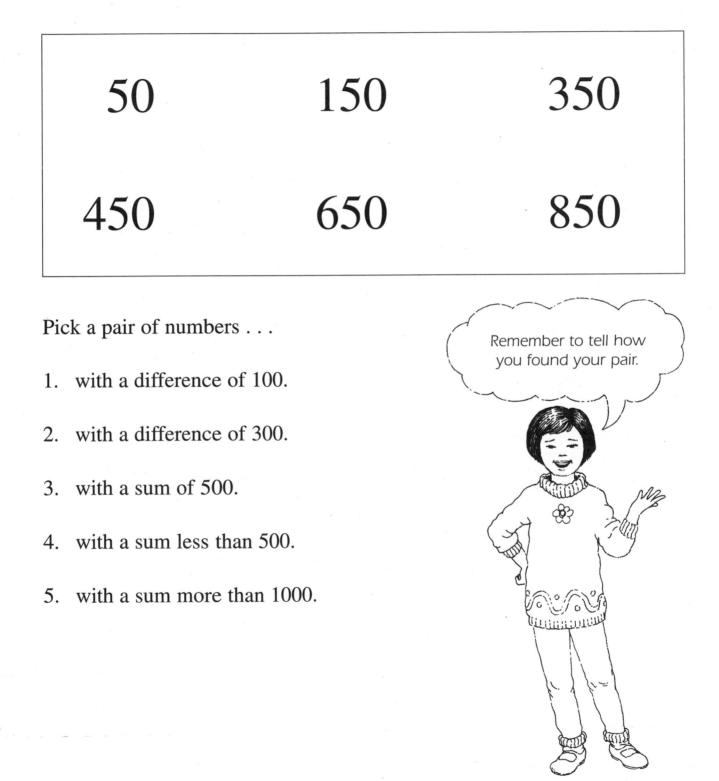

How Did You Find Them?

$0.50	$1.50	$3.50
$4.50	$6.50	$8.50

Pick a pair of numbers . . .

1. with a difference of $1.00.

2. with a difference of $3.00.

3. with a sum of $5.00.

4. with a sum less than $5.00.

5. with a sum more than $10.00.

Remember to tell how you found your pair.

Watch Those Signs!

Number Sense Focus

- Multiple representation
- Mental computation

Number Focus

- Activities 1–5: Whole numbers

Mathematical Background

Thoughtful reflection about the numbers and operations in a computation is a crucial number sense skill. Computations with the same numbers in the same order can produce different results when the operations are changed: $6 + 2 = 8, 6 - 2 = 4, 6 \times 2 = 12, 6 \div 2 = 3$. Students also need to recognize the importance of order of operations. The rules for order of operations require that operations in parentheses be done first, then multiplication and division from left to right, then addition and subtraction. The expressions $2 + 3 \times 4$ and $(2 + 3) \times 4$ look similar but produce quite different results (14 or 20).

Using the Activities

These activities encourage students to examine numbers and operations carefully. (In Activities 3–5, it is possible for students to introduce negative integers by using subtraction.)

1. As a warm-up, ask students to make a number sentence from 1, 2, and 3, in that order, to produce different results. For example:

$(1 + 2) \div 3 = 1$	$(1 \times 2) + 3 = 5$	$1 + 2 + 3 = 6$
$1 + (2 \times 3) = 7$	$(1 + 2) \times 3 = 9$	$1 \times 2 \times 3 = 6$

    List the expressions on the board. Although it is not necessary to put parentheses around the multiplication expressions as done above, it helps call attention to the groupings. Without parentheses $1 + 2 \times 3 = 7$, but $1 + 2 \div 3 \neq 1$.

2. In Activity 1, ask students to pick *any three* numbers and tell how they are related. For example, one student might pick 2, 3, and 5 and say $5 - 3 = 2$, and another might say $5 = 3 + 2$; list both relationships on the board. Use Activity 2 in a similar way.

3. In Activity 3, make a list of the different ways students find to make the numbers 0, 2, and 10. As they share the results they find between 0 and 10, challenge other students to find out how each result was made.

4. Activities 4 and 5 provide more opportunities to explore the order of operations and mental computation. Make a class list of solutions for the list of 5s so everyone can see the many answers possible. You may want students to work in small groups on the last activity. They can make records of their numbers and the solutions for display. Use Activity 5 to try different numbers.

Solutions

Some possibilities for each activity are given here.

Activity 1

$5 - 2 = 3, 5 = 2 + 3, 2 \times 3 = 6, 6 - 5 = 1, 2 + 1 = 3$

Activity 2

$24 \div 6 = 4, 24 \div 4 = 6, 4 \times 6 = 24, 20 + 4 = 24, 20 \div 4 = 5$

Activity 3

1. $(1 + 2 - 3) \times 4 = 0, 1 - 2 - 3 + 4 = 0$
2. $1 + 2 + 3 - 4 = 2, 1 \times 2 \times 3 - 4 = 2$
3. $1 + 2 + 3 + 4 = 10, 1 \times 2 \times 3 + 4 = 10$
4. $1 \times 2 - 3 + 4 = 3, 1 + 2 - 3 + 4 = 4, 1 - 2 + 3 + 4 = 6$
5. $(1 + 2) \times 3 \times 4 = 36$

Activity 4

1. $5 + 5 - 5 - 5 = 0, 5 + 5 + 5 + 5 = 20, 5 \times 5 - 5 - 5 = 15$
2. $(5 + 5) \times (5 + 5) = 100$

Extending the Activities

• •

- Challenge students to make all the numbers they can using the digits of the current year in order.

Watch Those Signs!

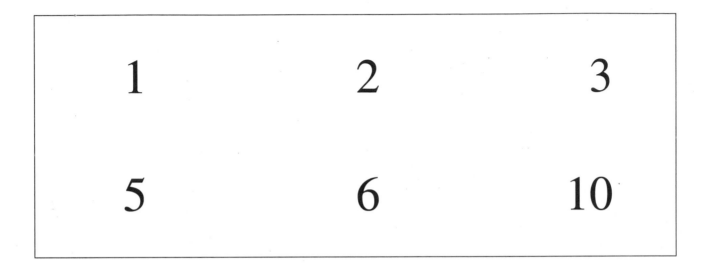

1	2	3
5	6	10

Pick three numbers from the box.

Use the three numbers to show a relationship.

Make a list of the different relationships you find.

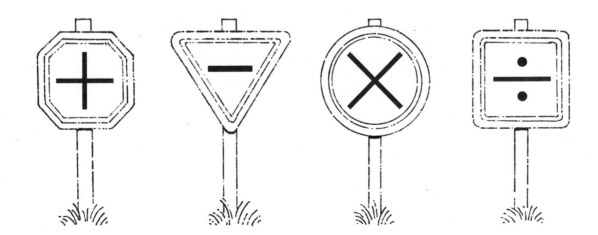

Watch Those Signs!

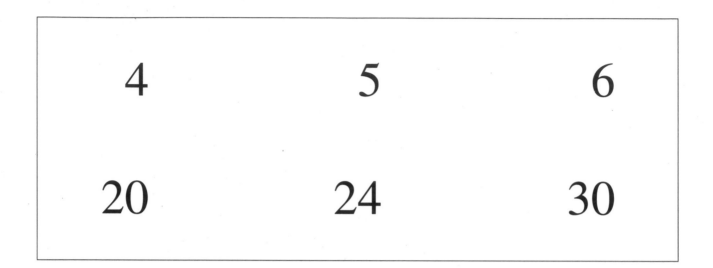

4	5	6
20	24	30

Pick any three numbers from the box.

Use the three numbers any way you like to show a relationship.

Make a list of the different relationships you find.

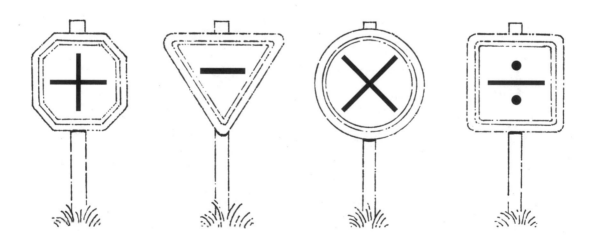

Watch Those Signs!

1	2	3	4

Use the numbers in the box in the order shown.

1. Put signs between the numbers to make 0.

2. Put signs between the numbers to make 2.

3. Put signs between the numbers to make 10.

4. What other results can you make between 0 and 10?

5. What is the largest result you can make?

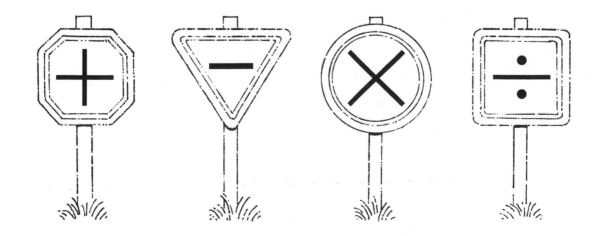

Watch Those Signs!

| 5 | 5 | 5 | 5 |

1. Make a list of the different numbers you can make with four 5s.

2. Try to make 100 with four 5s.

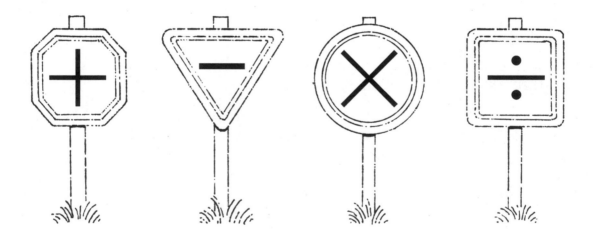

Number SENSE / Grades 3–4

Watch Those Signs!

＿＿＿＿　＿＿＿＿　＿＿＿＿　＿＿＿＿

Put any four digits in the spaces.

Then, add signs between them.

What is the result?

Change the signs to make a different result.

Make a list of all the results you find.

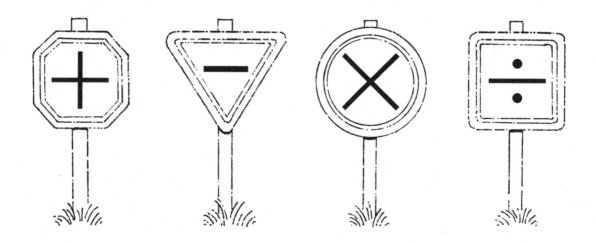

EXPERIENCE 15

• •

Number This Name

Number Sense Focus

- Multiple representation
- Relative size

Number Focus

- Activities 1–3: Whole numbers

Mathematical Background

• •

Just as knowing the names for animals is important for identifying and discussing them, knowing common number names helps us communicate mathematical ideas intelligently and effectively. Mathematical concepts may be encountered in many settings, but the appropriate terms must eventually be connected to the concepts to harness their full power.

Using the Activities

• •

In these activities, the class explores everyday and esoteric mathematical vocabulary. You may want to have a dictionary handy.

1. In Activities 1 and 2, ask students to identify the number associated with each term.

2. In Activity 3, explore each part as a class. Explain the meanings of terms with which they are unfamiliar, such as *hexapod* (having six feet) and *pentathlon* (an athletic contest with five events). Ask students to identify the number associated with each prefix; recognizing common prefixes provides useful clues to word meanings.

Solutions

Activity 1

twins, 2; triplets, 3; quadruplets, 4; quintuplets, 5; sextuplets, 6

Activity 2

soloist, 1; duet, 2; trio, 3; quartet, 4; quintet, 5; sextet, 6; septet, 7; octet, 8

Activity 3

4. A, triangle; B, pentagon; C, octagon; D, quadrilateral; E, decagon; F, hexagon

Extending the Activities

- Ask students to write a sentence or story that uses some of the new words in a meaningful way.

- Talk to the class about other number prefixes. For example, *hepta* and *septa* are both prefixes meaning seven.

- As a class, make a list of some of the prefixes used with metric measures.

Number This Name

quintuplets

quadruplets

twins

sextuplets

triplets

What number corresponds to each word above?

2   3   4   5   6

Number SENSE / Grades 3–4

Number This Name

sextet

duet

trio

soloist

quartet

quintet

septet

octet

What number corresponds to each word above?

$$1 \quad 2 \quad 3 \quad 4 \quad 5 \quad 6 \quad 7 \quad 8$$

Number This Name

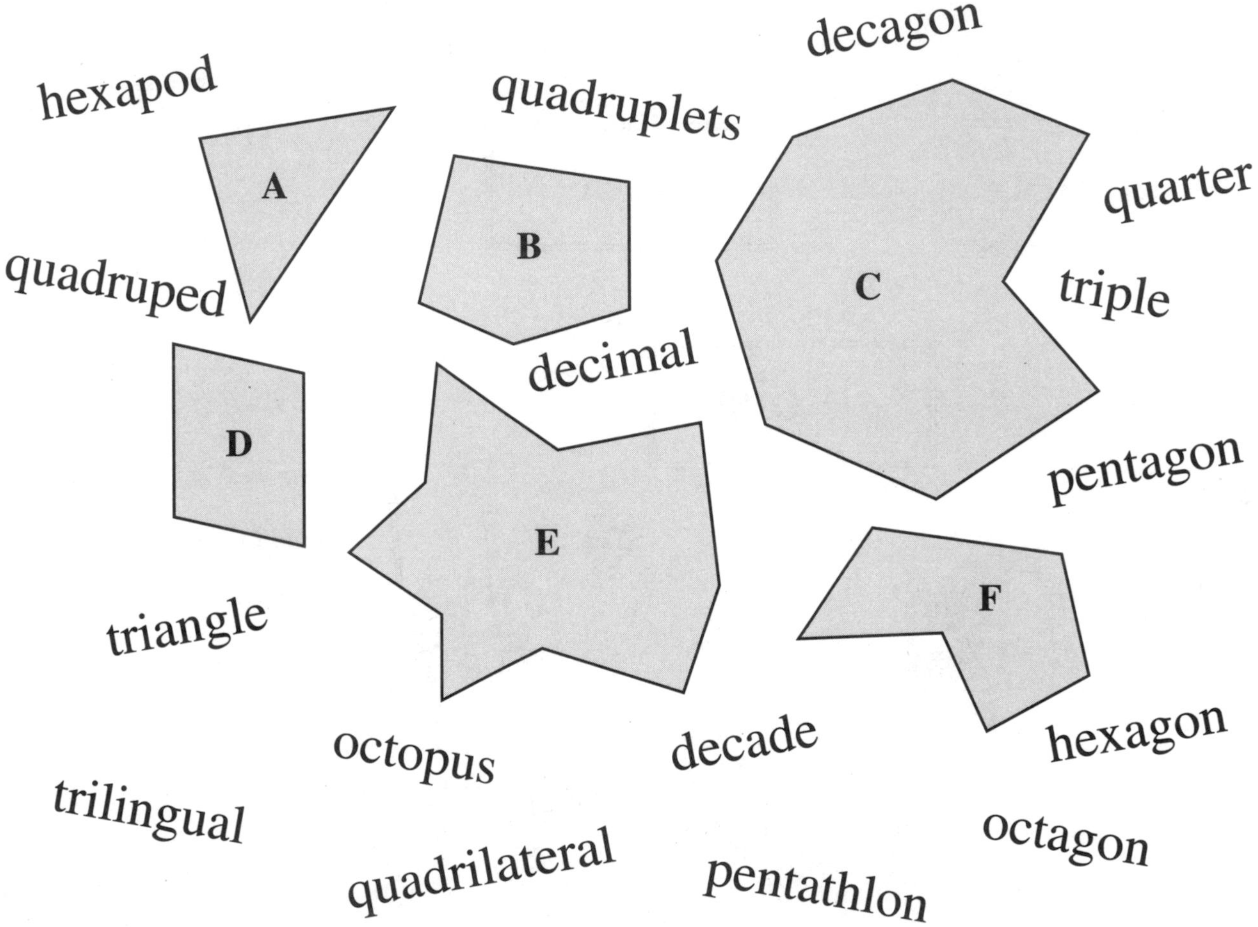

quart

decagon

hexapod

quadruplets

A

B

C

quadruped

decimal

quarter

triple

D

E

F

triangle

pentagon

octopus

decade

hexagon

trilingual

octagon

quadrilateral

pentathlon

1. Find five words with the same prefix. What does this prefix mean?

2. Find other pairs of words with the same prefix. What does each prefix mean?

3. Tell what each word means.

4. Match a word to each polygon.

Exploring Number Relationships

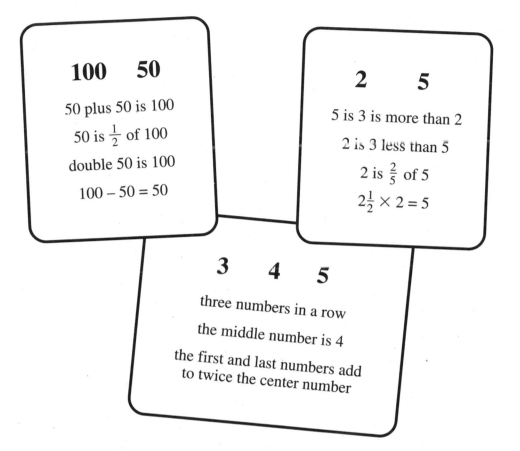

Every number is related to other numbers in many ways. The recognition of multiple relationships among numbers is one of the hallmarks of people with good number sense. In mental computation, the numbers 10 or 100 are particularly useful, as are compatible numbers.

Recognizing relationships among numbers often makes a calculation simpler. For example, we can reason about 15×4 in many ways:

- $4 = 2 \times 2$, so $15 \times 4 = 15 \times 2 \times 2$, which is the same as $30 \times 2 = 60$.

- $15 = 13 + 2$, and $13 \times 4 = 52$ (like a deck of cards), plus 8 is 60.

- $15 \times 2 = 30$, and double 30 is 60.

The greater the number of relationships among numbers that are recognized, the greater the number of choices that are available.

Number relationships are also used in estimation. For example, noticing the relationship between each number and 50 makes it possible to estimate 47 + 49 as less than 100 easily and confidently. Relationships also exist among sequences of numbers. For example, 2, 4, 6, 8, . . . and 2, 4, 8, 16, . . . are two forms of growth that demonstrate regular relationships between successive numbers. Recognizing such patterns helps us to identify trends and regularities in data and to notice when a number seems to be out of place because it does not fit the pattern.

These activities encourage students to explore number relationships and to take advantage of the relationships they observe.

Addition and Subtraction

Number Sense Focus

- Number relationships
- Mental computation

Number Focus

- Activities 1–3: Whole numbers

Mathematical Background

When we compute mentally, we constantly discover and use relationships among numbers. For example, when adding 27 and 15, we may think of 15 as 3 + 12 and so calculate 30 + 12.

Using the Activities

These activities encourage students to spot both simple and more complex addition and subtraction connections among sets of three numbers.

1. The numbers in Activity 1 lend themselves to simple addition and subtraction relationships, such as 3 + 5 = 8, 11 + 13 = 24, and 19 − 14 = 5. Show the first group of numbers, and invite students to choose three numbers to connect. Offer an example of your own.

2. Invite individuals to name their three numbers and state the relationship. Ask whether other students connected the same three numbers with a different relationship. Make a class list of the relationships, and add more relationships as students think of them. For example:

24 − 16 = 8	3 + 8 = 11	5 + 8 = 13	14 − 3 = 11
24 − 5 = 19	8 + 11 = 19	21 − 18 = 3	5 + 16 = 21

Many relationships exist for each set of numbers in this experience.

3. Use the other activities in the same way.

Extending the Activities

• •

- Allow students two or three minutes to write as many connections as they can for sets of three numbers in a given group of numbers.

- Challenge students to create a set of 10 numbers with as many interesting relationships as possible.

- Ask students to find relationships among four numbers in each group. For example, in Activity 1, one relationship is $3 + 13 = 21 - 5$.

Addition and Subtraction

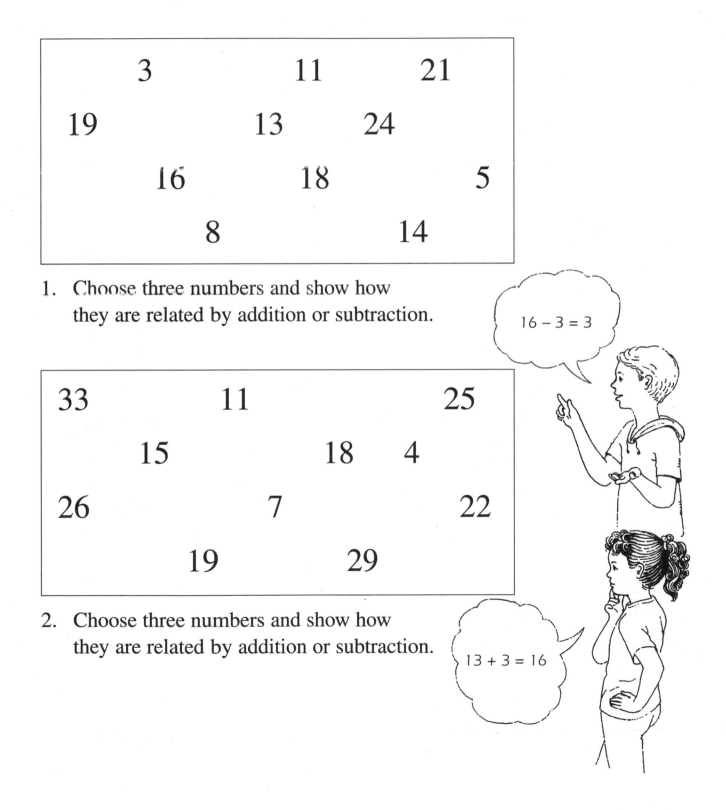

3	11	21
19	13	24
16	18	5
8	14	

1. Choose three numbers and show how they are related by addition or subtraction.

16 – 3 = 3

33	11	25
15	18	4
26	7	22
19	29	

2. Choose three numbers and show how they are related by addition or subtraction.

13 + 3 = 16

Addition and Subtraction

2	8	31
34 23	21	5
39	29	13
26	18	

1. Choose three numbers and show how
   they are related by addition or subtraction.

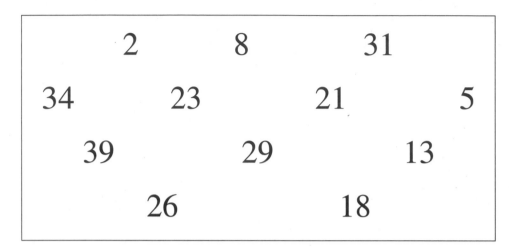

18 + 5 = 23

7	54	25
36	40	32
43	29	18
47	11	

2. Choose three numbers and show how
   they are related by addition or subtraction.

Addition and Subtraction

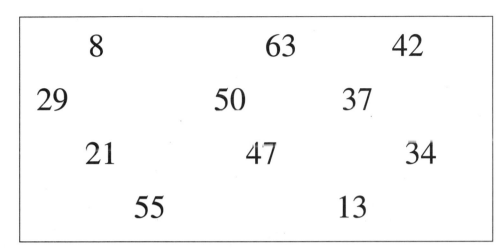

1. Choose three numbers and show how
   they are related by addition or subtraction.

55 − 42 = 13

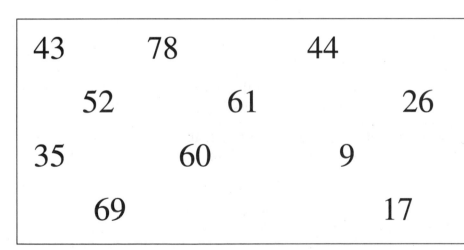

2. Choose three numbers and show how
   they are related by addition or subtraction.

EXPERIENCE 17

Multiplication and Division

Number Sense Focus

- Number relationships
- Mental computation

Number Focus

- Activities 1–3: Whole numbers

Mathematical Background

Recognizing relationships among numbers is useful in multiplication and division. For example, when multiplying 15 by 12, we may think of 15 as $10 + 5$ and calculate $10 \times 12 = 120$ and $5 \times 12 = 60$, giving a result of 180.

Using the Activities

These activities encourage students to discover multiplication and division connections among sets of three numbers.

1. Show the first set of numbers in Activity 1, and invite students to choose three numbers to connect using multiplication or division. Offer an example of your own.

2. Invite individual students to name their three numbers and state the relationship. Ask whether other students found other relationships for the numbers. List all the relationships, adding additional relationships as students find them. For example:

$2 \times 3 = 6$	$8 \div 4 = 2$	$12 \div 3 = 4$	$4 \times 6 = 24$
$8 \times 12 = 96$	$48 \div 6 = 8$	$32 \div 8 = 4$	$72 \div 12 = 6$

   Many possibilities exist for each set of numbers.

3. Encourage students to look for patterns in the class list, such as $12 \times 4 = 48$ and $48 \div 4 = 12$, and $12 \times 3 = 36$ and $36 \div 3 = 12$.

4. Activities 2 and 3 include extended basic facts such as $20 \times 30 = 600$.

Extending the Activities

- Allow students two or three minutes to write as many connections as they can for sets of three numbers in a given group of numbers.

- Challenge students to create a set of 10 numbers with many multiplication and division relationships. You may wish to include the operations of addition and subtraction as well.

- Ask students to find relationships among four numbers in each group. For example, in Activity 1, one relationship is $2 \times 12 = 4 \times 6$.

Multiplication and Division

144	3	48	72
32	36	18	12
24	16	6	8
2	96		4

1. Choose three numbers above, and show how they are related by multiplication or division.

48 ÷ 4 = 12
or
4 × 12 = 48

5	90	45	15	6
2	12	180		120
18	30	10	50	60
75	20	3		150

2. Choose three numbers above, and show how they are related by multiplication or division.

Number SENSE / Grades 3–4

Multiplication and Division

200	1000	10	250
40	2	400	500
100	20	50	5

1. Choose three numbers above, and show how they are related by multiplication or division.

$40 \times 5 = 200$

180	600	72	10	300
24	120	30	50	60
6	20	150	2	240
	12	360	5	

2. Choose three numbers above, and show how they are related by multiplication or division.

Multiplication and Division

75	720	300	12	180
240	36	100	48	60
3	80		45	15
20	5	540		4

1. Choose three numbers above, and show how they are related by multiplication or division.

250	3	500	90	30
45	2250	75	15	150
5	750	1500	450	
1350		300	10	50

$60 \div 12 = 5$

2. Choose three numbers above, and show how they are related by multiplication or division.

What Did I Buy?

Number Sense Focus

- Number relationships
- Mental computation

Number Focus

- Activities 1–3: Whole numbers, decimals

Mathematical Background

Mental computation is greatly enhanced by the recognition of compatible numbers—for example, pairs of numbers that total a multiple of 10 or 100, such as 22 and 28, or 36 and 64. In this experience, students may use the bridging-100 strategy for adding numbers such as 88 and 34 by reasoning, for example, that 88 and 12 make 100, plus 22 is 122.

Using the Activities

In these activities, students focus on finding compatible money values totaling $1.00 or $2.00.

1. In Activity 1, all values are multiples of 5 cents. As students locate pairs of stamps that total $1.00, ask how they calculated the sum; for example:

   - "I chose the 65¢ and 35¢ stamps. 65 and 5 is 70, and 30 more is 100."

   - "I chose the 75¢ and 25¢ stamps. 70 and 20 is 90, and 5 and 5 is 10. 90 plus 10 is 100."

2. In Activity 2, students again find pairs of stamps with a value of $1.00, but the values are not multiples of 5 cents.

3. In Activity 3, students find pairs of stamps with a value of $2.00.

Extending the Activities

• •

- Name pairs of stamps at random, and ask students for their total value.

- Challenge students to give the total value of all the stamps in each activity.

- Invite students to create their own sets of stamps for this activity.

- Say a number between 1 and 99, and ask students to name its pair—the number that, when added to yours, gives a sum of 100.

What Did I Buy?

Find a pair of stamps with a value of $1.00.

What Did I Buy?

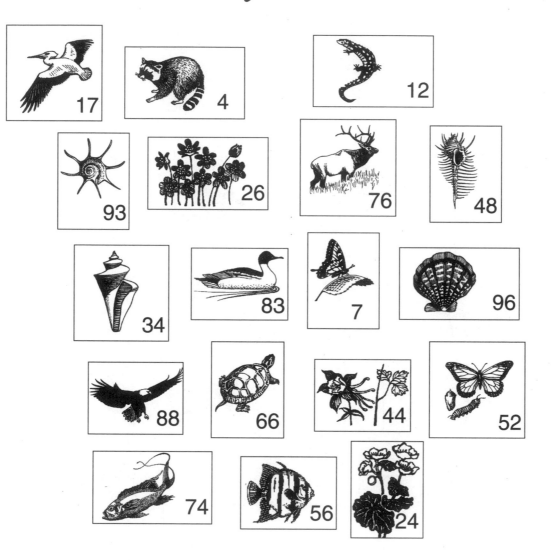

Find a pair of stamps with a value of $1.00.

What Did I Buy?

Find a pair of stamps with a value of $2.00.

EXPERIENCE 19

• •

What Number Am I?

Number Sense Focus

- Number relationships
- Multiple representation

Number Focus

- Activities 1–3: Whole numbers

Mathematical Background

• •

Any number can be described in many ways. For example, 24 is 20 + 4, the number of hours in a day, and two dimes and four pennies. Part of good number sense is recognizing different ways of expressing numbers and their characteristics.

Using the Activities

• •

In these activities, students are asked to name a whole number that satisfies certain clues.

1. As a warm-up, ask students to tell you some things about the number 10. For example, it is less than 20, it is even, it has 5 as a factor, and it equals 3 + 7. Create a list of their ideas.

2. Put students in teams of two or four. Reveal the first puzzle in Activity 1 for teams to consider as a group. Ask that they agree on one answer for the set of clues and be prepared to justify it.

3. Let groups share their answers. Note that some of the puzzles have more than one correct answer.

4. Activity 2 uses the word *prime*. If your students do not know that word, tell them that a *prime number* has only two factors, 1 and the number itself. Give them examples of prime numbers and numbers that are not prime.

Solutions

Activity 1

1. 5
2. 14, 28, 42, or . . .
3. 6 or 12
4. 19
5. 9, 25, or 49
6. 72

Activity 2

1. 24
2. 32
3. 30, 40, 50, or . . .
4. 11
5. 39
6. 16

Activity 3

1. 66
2. 42 or 62
3. 25, 115, 205, or . . .
4. 81, 144, 225, or . . .
5. 11 or 31
6. 50

Extending the Activities

• Have teams make up their own number puzzles and exchange them.

• Ask students to identify unnecessary clues.

What Number Am I?

1	2	3	4	5	6	7	8	9
11	12	13	14	15	16	17	18	19
21	22	23	24	25	26	27		
31	32	33	34	35	36			
41	42	43	44					

1. I am between 1 and 20.
   I am less than 10.
   I am odd.
   I am prime.
   I am a factor of 20.
   What number am I?

2. I am more than 10.
   I am even.
   I am a multiple of 7.
   What number am I?

3. I am between 5 and 15.
   I am not odd.
   3 is one of my factors.
   What number am I?

4. I am more than 10.
   My digits add to 10.
   I am less than 20.
   What number am I?

5. I am odd.
   I am less than 50.
   I am a square number.
   What number am I?

6. I am even.
   My two digits add to 9.
   My digits differ by 5.
   What number am I?

What Number Am I?

1	2	3	4	5	6	7	8	9
11	12	13	14	15	16	17	18	19
21	22	23	24	25	26	27		
31	32	33	34	35	36			
41	42	43	44					

1. I am between 1 and 50.
   My ones digit is 4.
   My digits total an even number.
   My digits are different.
   What number am I?

2. My digits total 5.
   I am even.
   I am less than 100.
   I am a multiple of 4.
   What number am I?

3. I am a multiple of 5.
   I am even.
   I am greater than 25.
   What number am I?

4. My digits are the same.
   I am odd.
   I am prime.
   What number am I?

5. I am less than 40.
   My digits are both multiples of 3.
   I am 1 less than a multiple of 5.
   What number am I?

6. I am a square number.
   I am a multiple of 2.
   I am less than 100.
   My digits add to less than 9.
   What number am I?

What Number Am I?

1	2	3	4	5	6	7	8	9
11	12	13	14	15	16	17	18	19
21	22	23	24	25	26	27		
31	32	33	34	35	36			
41	42	43	44					

1. I am between 1 and 100.
   My digits are the same.
   I am even.
   I am a multiple of 3.
   What number am I?

2. I am a 2-digit number.
   My ones digit is 2.
   My tens digit is even.
   I am between 30 and 70.
   What number am I?

3. I am odd.
   My digits add to 7.
   I am a multiple of 5.
   What number am I?

4. I am a square number.
   I am more than 50.
   My digits total 9.
   What number am I?

5. I am a prime number.
   I am less than 40.
   I am 1 more than a multiple of 5.
   What number am I?

6. I am not odd.
   I am not more than 50.
   I am not less than 50.
   What number am I?

From Here to There

Number Sense Focus

- Number relationships

Number Focus

- Activities 1–3: Whole numbers

Mathematical Background

Any pair of numbers can be related in an infinite number of ways. The ability to recognize and express a variety of relationships between numbers is a sign of good number sense.

Using the Activities

These activities invite students to explore ways to connect one number with another.

1. In Activity 1, explain that students are to find ways of getting from one number to the next using one addition and one subtraction. For example, the move from 10 to 31 could be accomplished in these ways:

   - $10 + 22 - 1 = 31$

   - $10 + 30 - 9 = 31$

   - $10 + 41 - 20 = 31$

2. Make a list of the students' suggestions. Invite them to comment on any patterns they see. (For example, the difference between the number added and the number subtracted is always 21.)

3. Now ask for suggestions for moving from 31 to 14, and so on around the ring of numbers.

4. Use Activities 2 and 3 in a similar way.

Extending the Activities

• •

- Have students create and work with their own rings of numbers.

- Challenge students to do an activity again, with an added restriction—for example, each solution must use the digit 5, or each solution must employ a two-digit number.

From Here to There

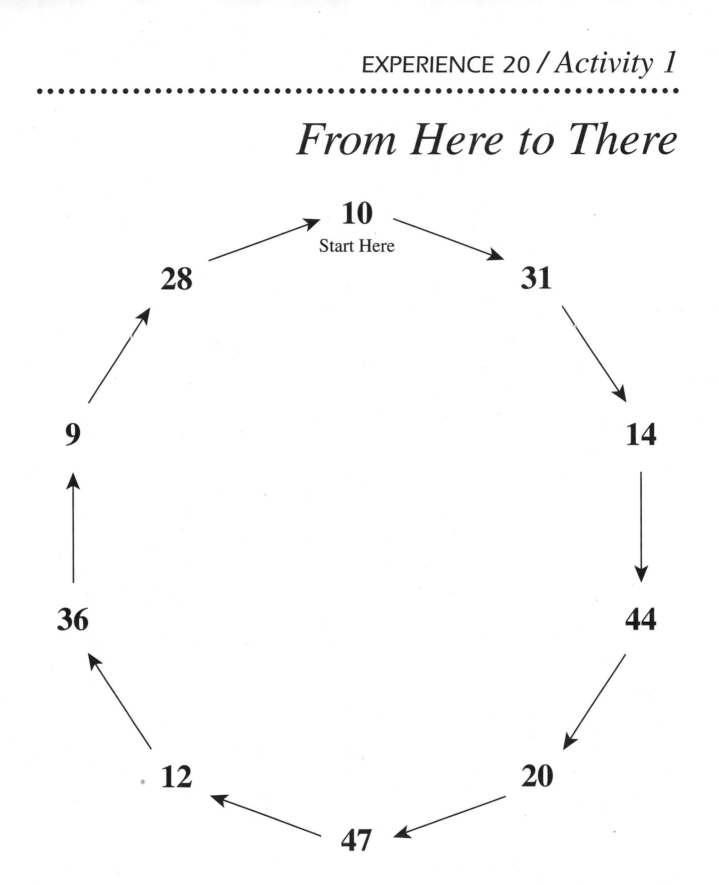

Move from one number to the next by using one addition
<u>and</u> one subtraction.

From Here to There

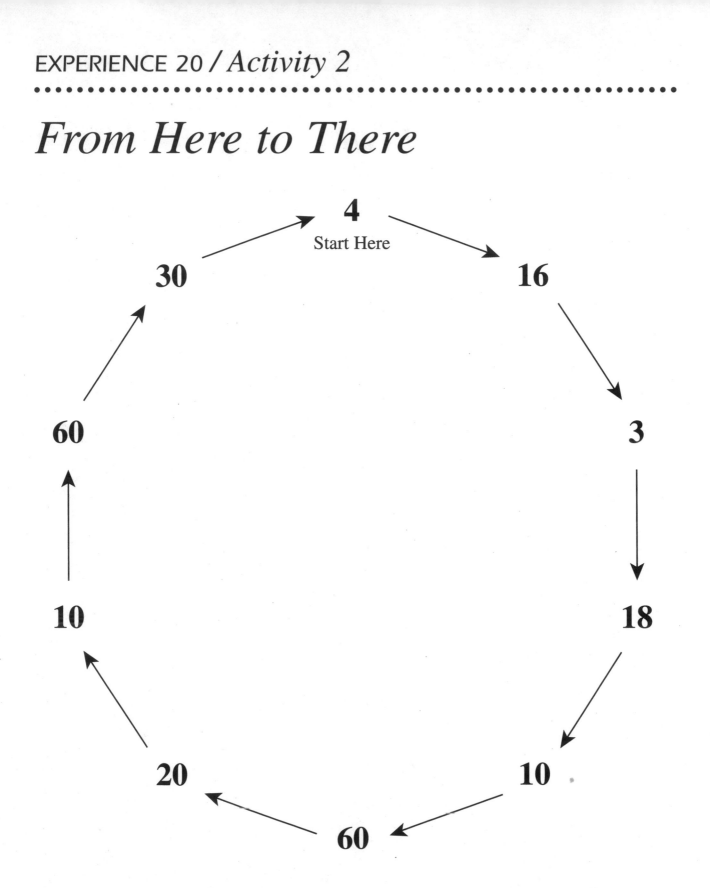

Move from one number to the next by using multiplication, division, or subtraction.

From Here to There

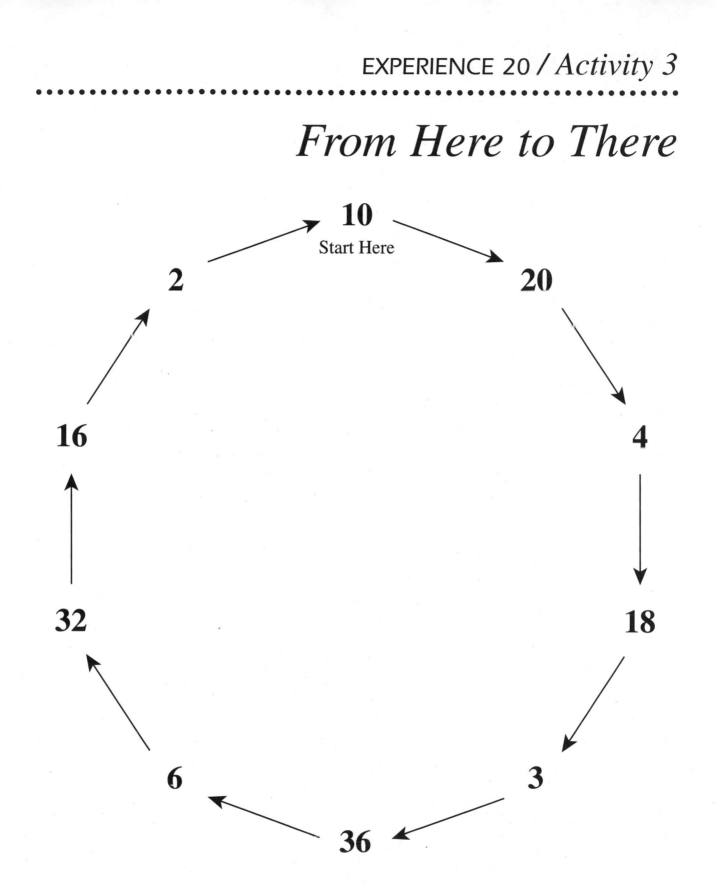

Move from one number to the next by using multiplication, division, <u>or</u> addition.

EXPERIENCE 21

Number Connections

Number Sense Focus

- Number relationships

Number Focus

- Activities 1–2: Whole numbers
- Activity 3: Whole numbers, decimals

Mathematical Background

Students need many experiences to work with the infinite variety of ways that numbers can be related.

Using the Activities

1. In Activity 1, choose a number between 20 and 100 to suit the abilities of your students and the calculations involved. Reveal one relationship at a time, or show the complete list and give students time to work through all 10 relationships. You might want to have students work in pairs, which will encourage them to discuss the relationships they see and the strategies they use.

2. The relationships in Activities 2 and 3 increase in difficulty. You may want to use Activities 1 and 2 several times, with different starting numbers, before presenting Activity 3.

Extending the Activities

- Have students make up their own sets of challenges.

Number Connections

My number is...

Name a number that . . .

1. is a little smaller than my number.

2. is a little larger than my number.

3. is 1 more than my number.

4. is twice my number.

5. is 10 times my number.

6. is 10 more than my number.

7. is half of my number.

8. is 100 more than my number.

9. is 25 more than my number.

10. when added to my number makes 100.

Number Connections

My number is...

Name a number that . . .

1. is 11 more than my number.

2. is 110 more than my number.

3. is 10 less than my number.

4. is about 3 times my number.

5. is about one third of my number.

6. is 20 more than twice my number.

7. is 100 times my number.

8. is 47 more than my number.

9. is a factor of my number.

10. is a multiple of my number.

Number Connections

My number is...

Name a number that . . .

1. is one tenth of my number.

2. is halfway between my number and 100.

3. is less than 1 greater than my number.

4. is about two thirds of my number.

5. is a little less than 10 times my number.

6. is smaller than 1 less than my number.

7. has a tens digit larger and a ones digit smaller than my number.

8. has a tens digit smaller and a ones digit larger than my number.

9. is very like my number, but different.

10. is very unlike my number.

EXPERIENCE 22

Name a Decimal

Number Sense Focus

- Number relationships
- Multiple representation

Number Focus

- Activities 1–3: Decimals

Mathematical Background

Students usually have plenty of opportunities to become familiar with the approximate size of the numbers up to 100 or 1000. However, they are often much less comfortable with approximations of decimal numbers—for example, knowing what decimals are approximately equal to 0.3 or what fractions, if any, exist between 0.1 and 0.2.

Using the Activities

These activities will strengthen students' grasp of relationships among decimals.

1. As a warm-up, ask the class to name a decimal larger than 0.5. Create a list of their suggestions to demonstrate the variety of answers. You might position each decimal offered on a number line as a visual model.

2. Have two to four students work together to write one answer for each clue. Each clue has an infinite number of solutions.

3. As a class, list several solutions for each clue. Have students explain how they found their answers. You may need to remind the class that whole numbers are also decimals; that is, 1 can be written as 1.0.

4. Follow a similar procedure for Activities 2 and 3.

Extending the Activities

- Have teams make up and exchange their own lists of clues.

- Ask students to search for examples of decimals in newspapers and to explain their meaning in the context.

Name a Decimal

Find an answer to fit each clue.
Show where your answer is on the number line.

| 0 | 0.2 | 0.4 | 0.6 | 0.8 | 1.0 | 1.2 | 1.4 | 1.6 | 1.8 | 2.0 |

Possible Answers

Clue 1   A decimal between 0 and 1.   _____

Clue 2   A decimal greater than 2.   _____

Clue 3   A decimal less than 0.1.   _____

Clue 4   A decimal close to zero.   _____

Clue 5   A decimal a little less than 1.   _____

Clue 6   Two decimals with a sum of 1.   _____

Clue 7   Two decimals with a sum of 0.8.   _____

Clue 8   Two decimals with a difference of 0.2.   _____

Clue 9   Two decimals with a sum between 2 and 3.   _____

Clue 10   Two decimals with a sum of 1.25.   _____

Clue 11   Two decimals with a sum of 0.75.   _____

Clue 12   Two decimals with a sum of 2.   _____

Name a Decimal

Find an answer to fit each clue.
Show where your answer is on the number line.

Possible Answers

Clue 1   A decimal between 0 and 0.10.   _____

Clue 2   A decimal between 0 and 0.1.   _____

Clue 3   A decimal between 0.1 and 0.2.   _____

Clue 4   A decimal that is about $\frac{1}{3}$.   _____

Clue 5   A decimal equal to one fourth.   _____

Clue 6   Two decimals between 0.2 and 0.3.   _____

Clue 7   Two decimals with a sum of 0.3.   _____

Clue 8   Two decimals with a sum of 0.1.   _____

Clue 9   Two decimals with a sum between 0.4 and 0.6.   _____

Clue 10   Two decimals whose difference is 0.1.   _____

Clue 11   Two decimals whose difference is 0.01.   _____

Clue 12   Two decimals with a sum between 1 and 2.   _____

Name a Decimal

Find an answer to fit each clue.
Show where your answer is on the number line.

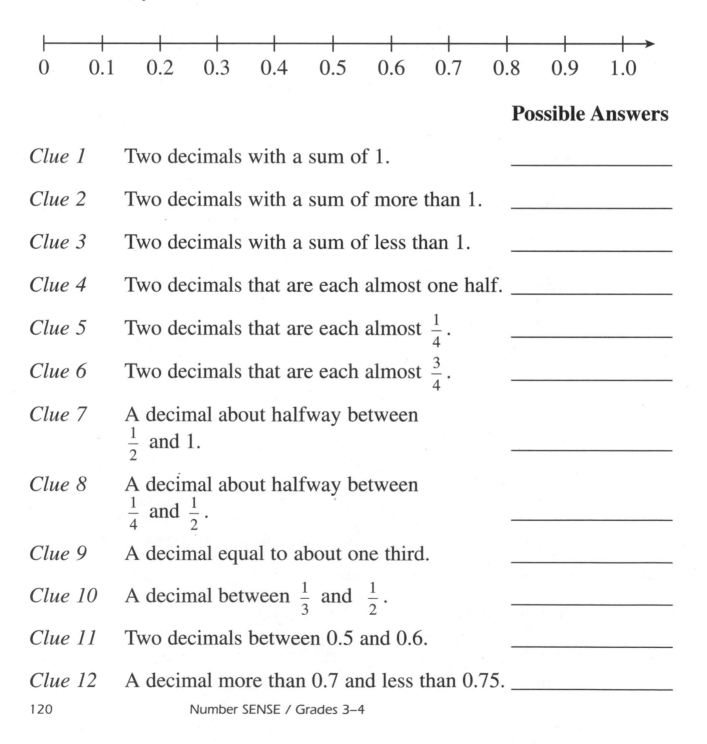

Possible Answers

Clue 1   Two decimals with a sum of 1.   _____

Clue 2   Two decimals with a sum of more than 1.   _____

Clue 3   Two decimals with a sum of less than 1.   _____

Clue 4   Two decimals that are each almost one half.   _____

Clue 5   Two decimals that are each almost $\frac{1}{4}$.   _____

Clue 6   Two decimals that are each almost $\frac{3}{4}$.   _____

Clue 7   A decimal about halfway between $\frac{1}{2}$ and 1.   _____

Clue 8   A decimal about halfway between $\frac{1}{4}$ and $\frac{1}{2}$.   _____

Clue 9   A decimal equal to about one third.   _____

Clue 10   A decimal between $\frac{1}{3}$ and $\frac{1}{2}$.   _____

Clue 11   Two decimals between 0.5 and 0.6.   _____

Clue 12   A decimal more than 0.7 and less than 0.75.   _____

Number *SENSE* / Grades 3–4

Exploring Relative Size

An awareness of the relative size of numbers requires a knowledge of strategies for relating the sizes of numbers, but it also involves personal judgment and decision making. For example, is A.D. 1800 relatively recent? A scholar of ancient history would likely answer this question differently from a scholar of contemporary history. In terms of a human life span, 1980 is recent to some people and ancient history to others. Personal knowledge, experience, and judgment are reflected in any decision about the relative size of numbers.

An understanding of the relative size of whole numbers and decimals depends on an understanding of place value. However, the relationships between whole numbers and decimals often result in confusion as students transfer experiences from one to the other. For example, place value quickly establishes that 49 is larger than 9; yet, for decimals such as 0.9 and 0.49, students often confuse the number of digits with their relative size. Strategies for comparing decimals include the technique of comparing them to critical benchmarks such as 0, 0.5, and 1.0.

Students also need practice with placing fractions in relation to one other. Strategies for comparing the sizes of fractions include understanding how fractions with equal numerators or denominators—such as $\frac{1}{5}$ and $\frac{1}{6}$, or $\frac{3}{7}$ and $\frac{4}{7}$—are related, and an ability to compare fractions to critical benchmarks such as 0, $\frac{1}{2}$, and 1.

Making 100 and More

Number Sense Focus

- Relative size
- Mental computation
- Estimation

Number Focus

- Activities 1–4: Whole numbers

Mathematical Background

The metric system is a natural context for exploring relative size. While working with scales based on powers of 10, students also employ estimation and compatible numbers.

Using the Activities

1. Cuisenaire® rods provide a nice model to support Activity 1. Show Bar A, and establish that its length is 10 cm or 100 mm. Then, show the other bars and ask: Which is the longest bar? the next longest? the shortest? Ask which pairs of bars will equal the 10-cm bar. Focus on relative size, rewarding evidence that students are joining bars to equal the length of Bar A.

2. Show the lengths at the bottom, and ask which bar goes with which length.

3. In Activity 2, the bars are marked in centimeters.

4. In Activity 3, the computations are a bit more difficult. Encourage students to use the markings to approximate the length of each bar.

5. In Activity 4, the graduated cylinders are marked, but the units are not indicated. This makes the activity more versatile: the cylinders could be 100 ml, 1000 ml (1 liter), or whatever is appropriate. Establish the total

volume, and ask students for examples of something the levels could represent. For a liter, the markings might indicate the amount of milk each student drank in one day. For a 100-ml total, the markings might be the amount of water each student could hold in their cupped hands. Ask students: Who filled their cylinder more than half? about half full? almost full? If the cylinder holds _____ (state an amount), about how much water does each person have?

Solutions

Activity 1

1. E and J, G and H, B and C, D and F, I and K
2. 10 mm, J; 20 mm, G; 30 mm, B; 40 mm, F; 50 mm, I and K; 60 mm, D; 70 mm, C; 80 mm, H; 90 mm, E

Activity 2

1. H and I, J and D, G and E, K and B, C and F
2. B, 3.5 cm; C, 4.5 cm; D, 8.5 cm; E, 7.5 cm; F, 5.5 cm; G, 2.5 cm; H, 0.5 cm; I, 9.5 cm; J, 1.5 cm; K, 6.5 cm

Activity 3

1. D and E, G and H, B and C, J and K, F and I
2. 9 mm, E; 14 mm, H; 25 mm, C; 28 mm, J; 48 mm, I; 52 mm, F; 72 mm, K; 75 mm, B; 86 mm, G; 91 mm, D

Activity 4

Approximate answers

Kendra, $\frac{4}{10}$; Shaqué, $\frac{65}{100}$; Danny, $\frac{9}{10}$; Kai, $\frac{3}{10}$; Joy, $\frac{55}{100}$

Extending the Activities

- Have students place their finger along a meter stick, name the location, and tell how many more centimeters are left on the meter stick.

- Tell students to imagine that you are filling a liter carton. Call out an amount in milliliters, and ask them to tell how many more milliliters will fill the carton.

Making 100 and More

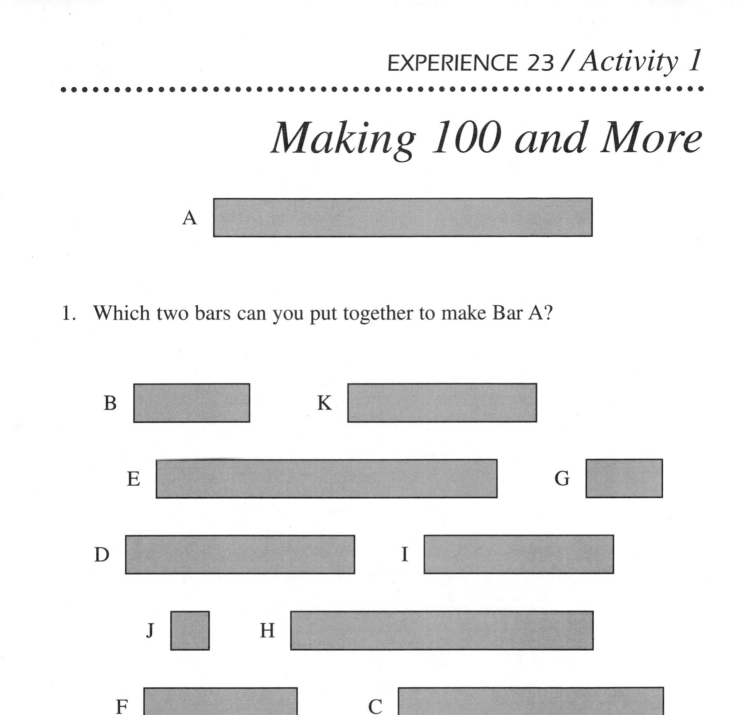

A

1. Which two bars can you put together to make Bar A?

B   K

E   G

D   I

J   H

F   C

2. Bar A is 100 mm long. Match these lengths to the other bars.

10 mm	20 mm	30 mm	40 mm	50 mm
60 mm	70 mm	80 mm	90 mm	

Making 100 and More

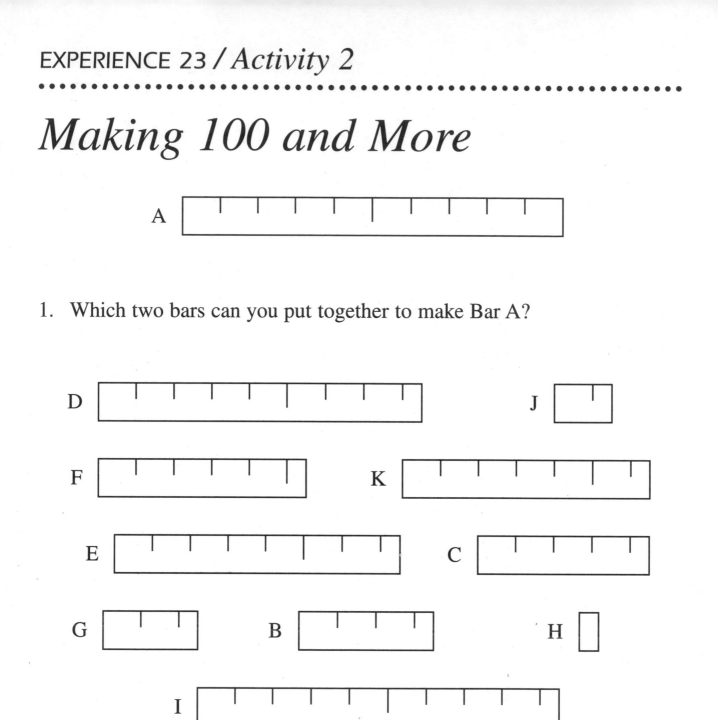

1. Which two bars can you put together to make Bar A?

2. What is the length of each bar?

Making 100 and More

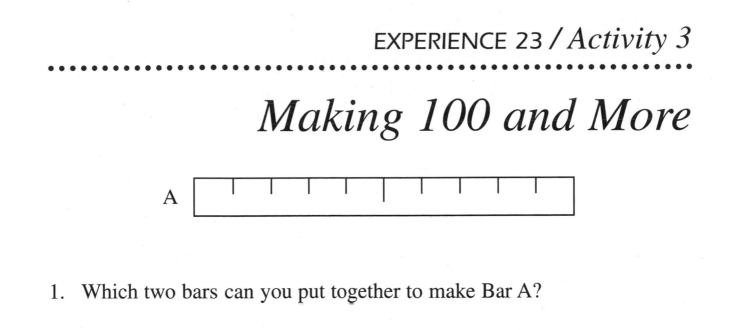

1. Which two bars can you put together to make Bar A?

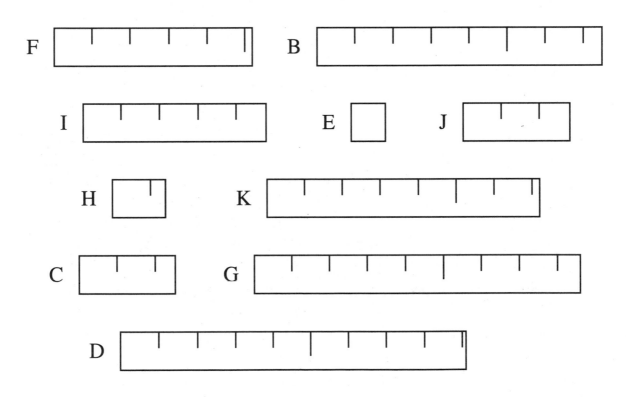

2. Match these lengths to the bars above.

9 mm	14 mm	25 mm	28 mm	48 mm
52 mm	72 mm	75 mm	86 mm	91 mm

Making 100 and More

Five students have five cylinders of water.

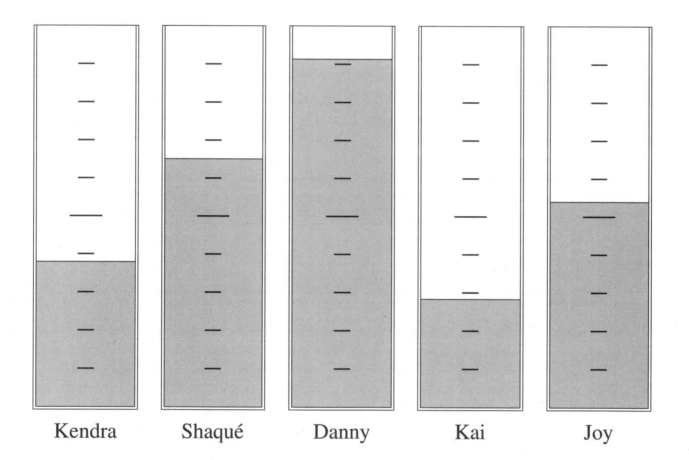

Kendra   Shaqué   Danny   Kai   Joy

About how full did each student fill the cylinder?

Can You See the Pattern?

Number Sense Focus

- Relative size
- Multiple representation
- Mental computation

Number Focus

- Activities 1–3: Whole numbers

Mathematical Background

Searching for and employing patterns among numbers helps students establish and develop a feeling for the relative size of numbers.

Using the Activities

In these activities, students will determine the approximate location of numbers on a grid by using patterns they see in the grid.

1. In Activity 1, explore each grid. Students are to imagine that the sequence of numbers continues. Discuss ways of finding the hidden numbers. Then, ask why the hidden values are different even though a similar pattern of squares is covered in each grid. (*Because the number of columns is different.*)

2. Ask students to imagine more rows being added to the 5-by-10 grid, then ask for the location of specific numbers. For example, in which row and column would 75 appear?

3. In Activity 2, ask students to determine the highest number that will appear on the 20-by-25 grid. *(500)* Have them share the strategies they used to answer your question. Next, call out numbers and ask for their location, or point out squares and ask which number belongs in that square. Focus on the patterns students employ as they answer your questions.

4. Follow a similar procedure for the 25-by-32 grid in Activity 3. (The highest number is 800.)

Solutions

Activity 1

1. 2, 14, 22, 23, 27, 28, 36, 41, 46, 49, 50
2. 2, 24, 42, 43, 52, 53, 71, 81, 91, 94, 95

Activity 2

10, 100, 101, 190, 200, 201, 301

Activity 3

5, 100, 105, 200, 201, 305, 500, 505, 600

Extending the Activities

● ●

- Have students draw their own number squares on grid paper and make up questions to challenge each other.

Can You See the Pattern?

What number is hidden under each gray square?

1.

1		3	4	5
6	7	8	9	10
11				

2.

1		3	4	5	6	7	8	9	10
11									

Can You See the Pattern?

What number is hidden under each gray square?

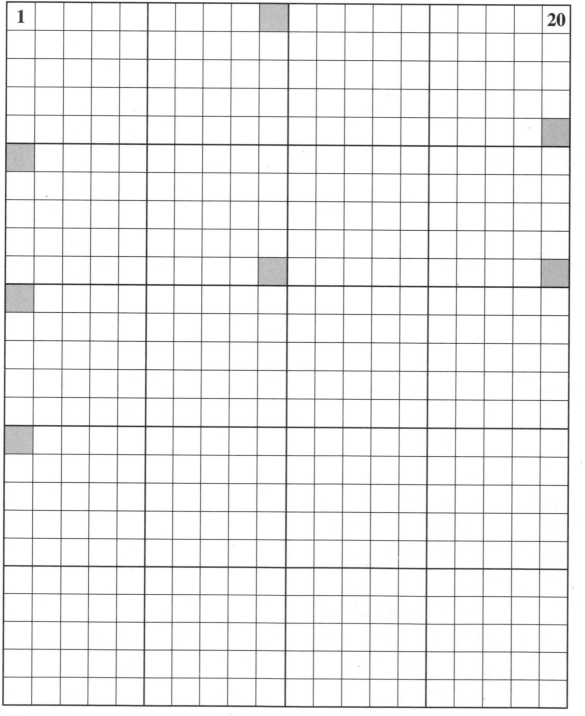

Number *SENSE* / Grades 3–4

Can You See the Pattern?

What number is hidden under each gray square?

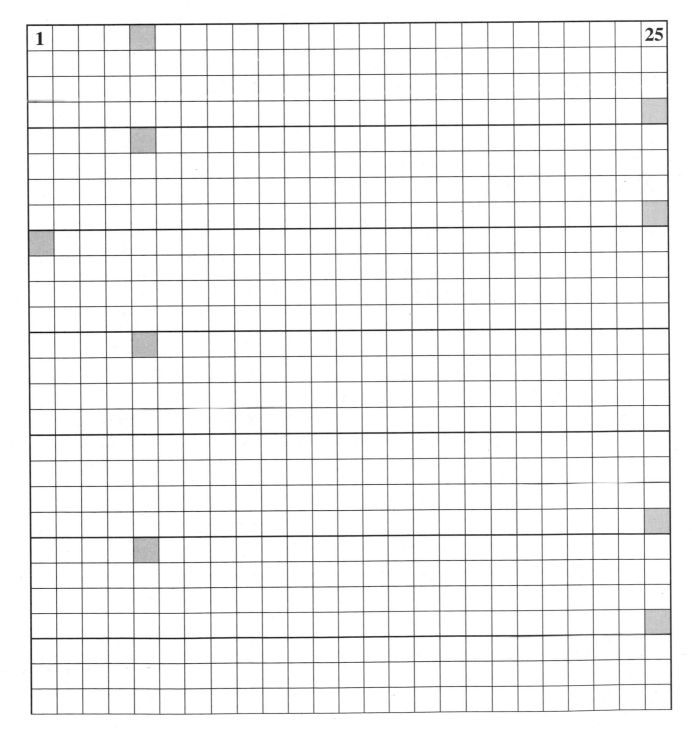

EXPERIENCE 25

• •

About Where Is It?

Number Sense Focus

- Relative size
- Measurement
- Estimation

Number Focus

- Activities 1–3: Whole numbers

Mathematical Background

• •

For the number line to be a meaningful and useful model for them, students need many experiences estimating values between designated points (interpolation) and estimating points beyond those shown (extrapolation). Benchmarks are often helpful for determining the relative size or location of values.

Using the Activities

• •

These activities offer perspectives of number lines that encourage thinking about the relative size of numbers. Because points near the middle and endpoints of number lines make good benchmarks, they are the focus of these activities.

1. As a warm-up, ask the students to count off and to each write their number on a stick-on note. Draw a line across the board, mark a starting point with 0, and ask one student at a time to place his or her number on the line. It may be necessary to move some numbers around as more students place their number.

2. In Activity 1, make sure students understand where 0 is located and to what value the arrow is pointing. As students address the questions, encourage them to share their thinking.

For example:

- "4 is twice as far from 0 as 2 is."

- "2 is halfway between 0 and 4."

- "Since 3 is less than 4, it goes about here."

Accept all reasonable estimates of the positions, focusing on *how* students explain their thinking.

3. Make sure students notice the similarity between the number lines in parts 1 and 2 and realize that one arrow points to 4 while the other points to 40.

4. In Activities 2 and 3, students must first understand where each arrow is pointing in order to get a feeling for the scale of each number line.

Extending the Activities

• •

- On an unmarked meter stick, show the endpoints of 0 and 100. Ask one student to place a finger on the meter stick, and ask another to estimate the value of that position.

About Where Is It?

1. About where is the arrow pointing?
    About where is 2? 3? 5?

    0 ⟍——————↑——————————————⟍ 10

2. About where is the arrow pointing?
    About where is 30? 50? 45?

    0 ⟍——————↑——————————————⟍ 100

3. About where is the arrow pointing?
    About where is 2? 24? 50?

    0 ⟍———↑———————————————————⟍ 100

4. About where is the arrow pointing?
    About where is 50? 102? 195?

    0 ⟍————————↑——————————————⟍ 200

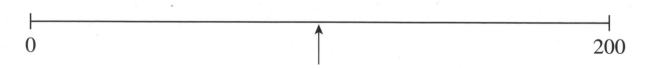

About Where Is It?

1. The arrow is pointing at 20.
   About where is 10? 22? 45?

   0

2. The arrow is pointing at 50.
   About where is 5? 55? 105?

   0

3. The arrow is pointing at 100.
   About where is 45? 98? 110?

   0

4. The arrow is pointing at 75.
   About where is 3? 73? 150?

   0

About Where Is It?

1. The arrow is pointing at 50.
   About where is 23? 49? 200?

   0

2. The arrow is pointing at 25.
   About where is 10? 26? 51?

   0

3. The arrow is pointing at 100.
   About where is 48? 101? 198?

   0

4. The arrow is pointing at 30.
   About where is 19? 41? 81?

   0

More About Where Is It?

Number Sense Focus

- Relative size
- Measurement
- Estimation

Number Focus

- Activities 1–3: Whole numbers

Mathematical Background
• •

Number-line models encourage students to use benchmarks and promote thinking about the relative size of numbers.

Using the Activities
• •

These activities use a "roller coaster" model of a number line.

1. In Activity 1, reveal the first number line. Make sure students see that 0 and 50 are located at either end of the hump of the "roller coaster." Ask students what value is at the highest point of the roller coaster. Encourage discussion that identifies this as the midpoint between 0 and 50. Then ask about where 46 is, and encourage students to explain their answers; for example:

   - "If you were at 46 on the roller coaster, you would roll to 50."

   - "46 is very close to 50."

   - "46 is almost to the right end."

2. Have one student ask the class where another value is on the number line, and encourage students to share their thinking as they offer locations.

3. Follow a similar procedure for Activities 2 and 3.

Extending the Activities

- Make a number line from 0 to 1000 on the classroom wall by putting together 10 meter sticks or using a metric tape measure. Call out a number between 0 and 1000, and have students point to its location as quickly as they can.

More About Where Is It?

About where is 46?

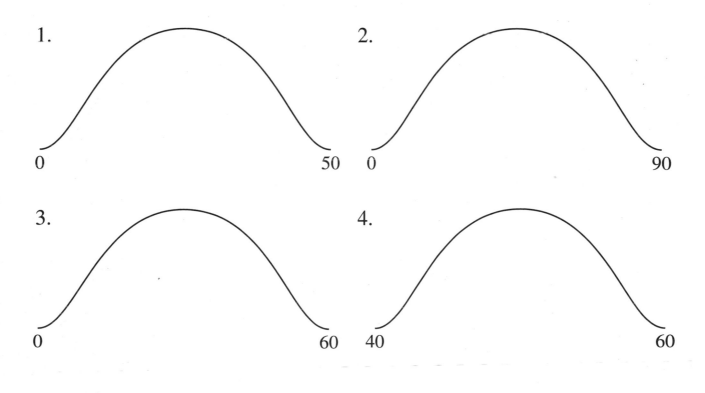

1.

0   50

2.

0   90

3.

0   60

4.

40   60

More About Where Is It?

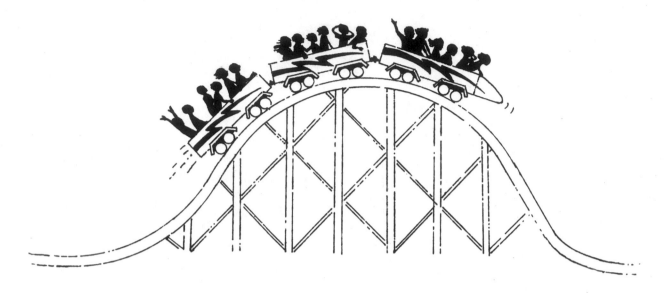

About where is 42?

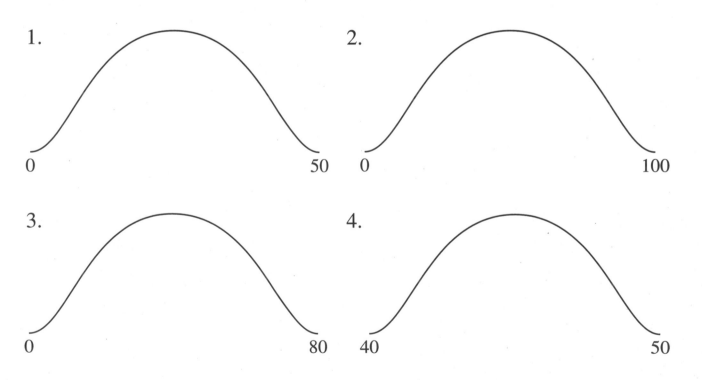

1.
0   50

2.
0   100

3.
0   80

4.
40   50

More About Where Is It?

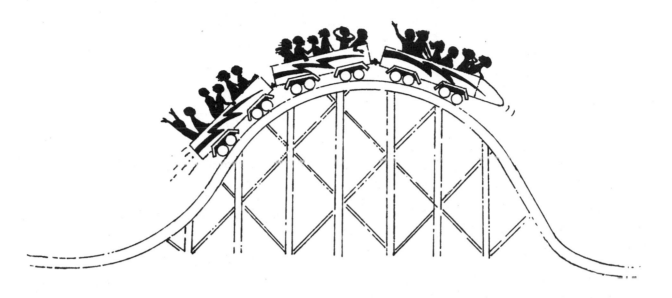

About where is 84?

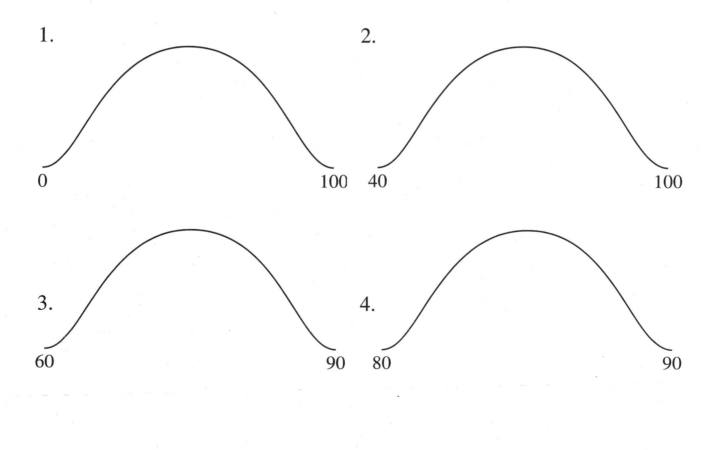

1.

0   100

2.

40   100

3.

60   90

4.

80   90

EXPERIENCE 27

Decimal Models

Number Sense Focus

- Relative size
- Estimation

Number Focus

- Activities 1–3: Decimals

Mathematical Background

Recognizing that a decimal is near 0, about $\frac{1}{2}$, or near 1 is important for ordering decimals and estimating decimal calculations. For example, by recognizing that the sum of two decimals that are near but less than $\frac{1}{2}$ must be less than 1, students can confidently estimate that a sum such as 0.44 + 0.47 must be less than 1.

Using the Activities

These activities encourage the development and use of decimal benchmarks.

1. As a warm-up, ask students for money amounts near a half dollar (for example, $0.48, $0.54, and $0.49). Write the amounts in different forms (48¢, $0.48, $\frac{48}{100}$). Students should realize that these are different representations of the same value.

2. Have students work in pairs on these activities. In Activity 1, ask students to match the nine grids with the nine decimals. Then, have them sort the decimals into the three groups: near 0, about $\frac{1}{2}$, and near 1.

3. In Activity 2, each pair should make a set of decimal cards (self-stick notes work nicely). As pairs sort the cards, ask them to justify their placements to each other. As you observe pairs working, have them describe, in general terms, how they know a particular decimal is nearest to 0, $\frac{1}{2}$, or 1.

4. As students work, help them explore patterns. Ask questions to focus their thinking:

- How do you know when a decimal is less than 0.5?

- Is the number of decimal places important for determining the size of a decimal?

- Which decimals are the hardest to put in order? Why?

You might connect the decimals to amounts of money, using real pennies to model the amounts.

5. In Activity 3, students work with sums of decimals.

Solutions

Activity 2

near 0: 0.04, 0.21, 0.09, 0.18
about $\frac{1}{2}$: 0.49, 0.59
near 1: 0.9, 0.82, 0.88, 0.90, 1.05

Activity 3

near 0: 0.03 + 0.08, 0.1 + 0.07, 0.09 + 0.01
about $\frac{1}{2}$: 0.5 + 0.05, 0.3 + 0.24, 0.23 + 0.29, 0.2 + 0.4, 0.39 + 0.13
near 1: 0.4 + 0.5, 0.13 + 0.74, 0.43 + 0.45, 0.1 + 0.8

Extending the Activities

- After students have ordered a set of decimals, invite them to write a decimal that falls between each pair of decimals.

- Put all the decimal cards in a bowl (add new ones if you like). Have students draw out two at a time, tell which decimal is larger, and explain their thinking.

Decimal Models

1. Match each grid with a decimal.

| 0.445 | 0.48 | 0.98 | 0.54 | 0.8 |

| 0.005 | 0.01 | 0.1 | 0.05 |

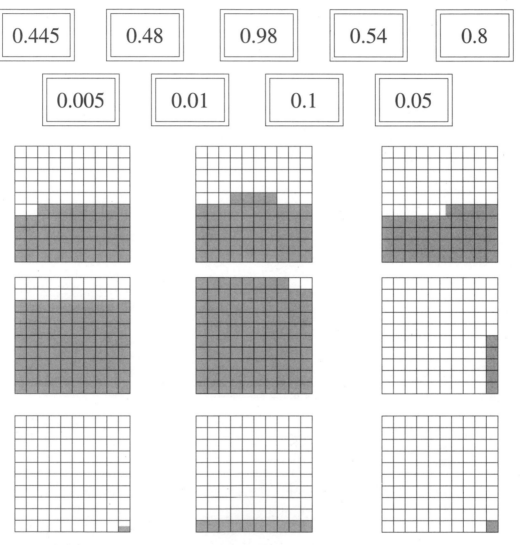

2. Sort the decimals into these three groups, and tell how you decided where each should go.

Near 0   **About $\frac{1}{2}$**   **Near 1**

Decimal Models

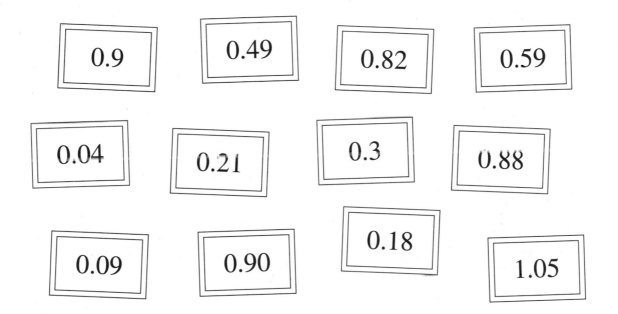

With your partner, make a set of decimal cards like these.

1. Sort your cards into three groups: Near 0, About $\frac{1}{2}$, and Near 1.

2. Make two new cards for each group.

3. Put all your cards in order by size.

Decimal Models

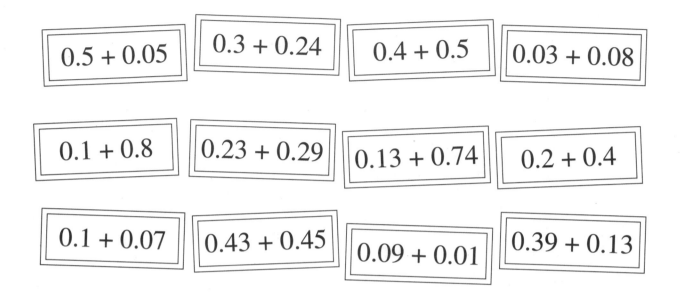

$$0.5 + 0.05 \qquad 0.3 + 0.24 \qquad 0.4 + 0.5 \qquad 0.03 + 0.08$$

$$0.1 + 0.8 \qquad 0.23 + 0.29 \qquad 0.13 + 0.74 \qquad 0.2 + 0.4$$

$$0.1 + 0.07 \qquad 0.43 + 0.45 \qquad 0.09 + 0.01 \qquad 0.39 + 0.13$$

With your partner, make a set of decimal cards like these.

1. Add the decimals on your cards, then sort the cards into three groups: Near 0, About $\frac{1}{2}$, and Near 1.

2. Make two new cards with sums for each group.

3. Put all your cards in order by size.

Number SENSE / Grades 3–4

Exploring Estimation

Estimates are useful when exact answers are impossible, unrealistic, or unnecessary. Measurements such as length, area, volume, distance, and time are approximations; they can be made more accurate by using a smaller unit, but they are always estimates. Estimation is about producing answers that are close enough to allow for good decisions without making extremely precise measurements or doing elaborate computations.

The first step in developing estimation skill is to learn to recognize whether a particular situation requires an exact answer or an estimate, and the degree of accuracy needed. When timing a slow-cooking casserole, half an hour more or less may not be crucial; with a microwave, seconds matter. Deciding whether to estimate and how closely to estimate promotes and rewards high-level mathematical thinking.

Estimation strategies are quite different from those we employ when an exact answer is needed. One valuable estimation technique is relating the estimate to a referent, or benchmark, that we know—such as the height of one story of a building, or the capacity of a milk carton. People with good number sense use a variety of personal benchmarks.

Research has shown that estimation employs mental computation, rewards flexible thinking, challenges students to think about numbers in ways that are meaningful for them, develops an awareness of multiple strategies, encourages a tolerance for error, and builds an appreciation of the power of inexact values in making decisions. The development of estimation skills helps dispel the one-right-answer syndrome often associated with exact computation. Research has also shown that students are often reluctant to estimate because they are more comfortable with exact answers. Thus they are unaware of how powerful estimation can be, both in and out of school.

The activities in this section will help students develop an appreciation for estimation and challenge them to think about what numbers to use and how to use them.

How Much?

Number Sense Focus

- Estimation
- Relative size

Number Focus

- Activities 1–2: Whole numbers
- Activity 3: Decimals

Mathematical Background

The ability to move between symbolic and pictorial representations of numbers is an important number sense skill.

Using the Activities

In these activities, which involve height and perimeter, numbers are related to an estimation of length.

1. Show the top row of pennies in Activity 1. Explain that the left-hand stack contains 100 coins. Invite students to estimate about how many pennies are in each of the other stacks. Repeat with the lower row of pennies.

2. In Activity 2, make sure the class understands that Pinecrest School has raised $1000 in all and that each column represents the amount of money raised after each of 10 months. Invite students to work in pairs to arrange the columns in order and to estimate the amount of money represented by each column. You may want to provide paper copies of the activities so students can cut out the columns and move them around. Or, cut up a transparency so the columns can be moved around on the overhead. Encourage a discussion of the strategies students used to estimate the height of each column.

3. In Activity 3, the circle is a ring of 100 pennies. Show the circle and make sure everyone agrees that darkened coin A is the 50¢ spot. Invite students to estimate the penny represented by the darkened coin in B–F.

Solutions

As these are estimates, accept a range of answers.

Activity 1

Barb, 50; Taiko, 25; Whitney, 10; Rustin, 75
Lee, 80; Karin, 30; Wyn, 60; Tamara, 95

Activity 2

Approximate amounts in order are F, $100; H, $200; B, $300; J, $350; A, $400; D, $550; G, $600; C, $700; I, $800, E, $1000.

Activity 3

A. 50
B. 25
C. 75
D. 15
E. 30
F. 94

Extending the Activities

• Show a plastic 2-liter bottle or a liquid measuring container partially filled with water, and ask students to estimate the amount of liquid in the container.

How Much?

Al has made a pile of 100 pennies. Estimate the number of pennies in each of the other students' piles.

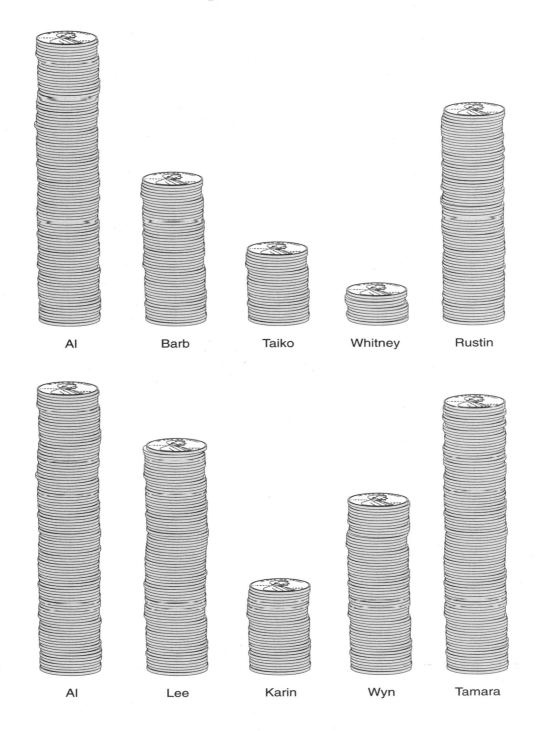

How Much?

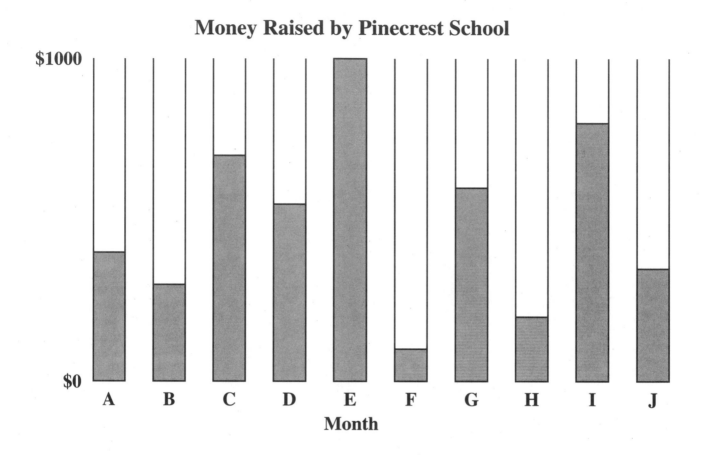

Money Raised by Pinecrest School

Pinecrest School is raising money to buy new computers. They raised $1000 in 10 months. The bars show how much money they had at the end of each month.

Put the bars in order. About how much money did Pinecrest School have at the end of each month?

How Much?

Here is a ring of 100 pennies. The first three pennies are numbered.
Which penny is in each position A–F.

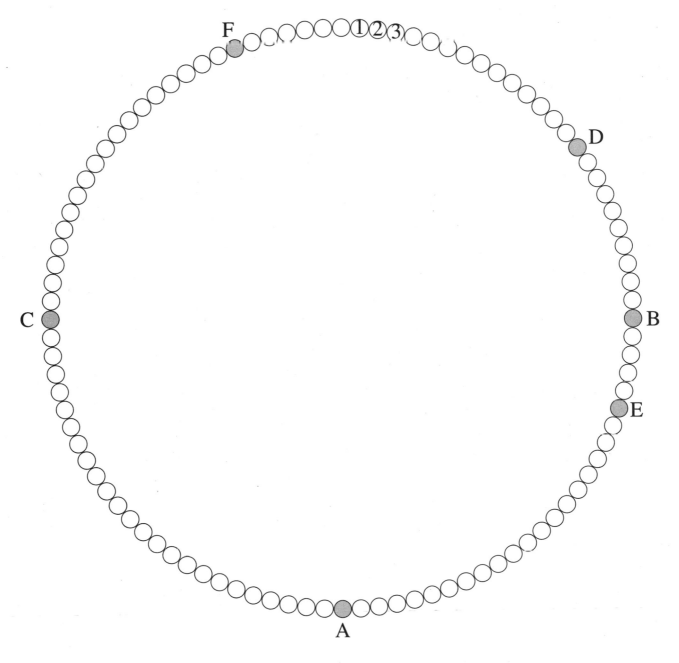

EXPERIENCE 29

•••••••••••••••••••••••••••

About How Many Are Shaded?

Number Sense Focus

- Estimation
- Relative size

Number Focus

- Activities 1–3: Whole numbers

Mathematical Background

•••••••••••••••••••••••••••••••

These activities offer students further experience in estimating quantities and making judgments that involve connecting pictures with numerical benchmarks.

Using the Activities

•••••••••••••••••••••••••••••••

In these activities, students estimate how many dots in a collection are shaded. They are challenged to do this not by counting but by visually surveying the collection of dots. These activities will generate a rich discussion as students share how they made their estimates.

1. In Activity 1, explain that you will show a picture of 50 dots for a few seconds. The students are to decide whether the number of shaded dots shown is more or less than half the total number of dots. If they think the number of shaded dots is more than 25, they will give a thumbs up. If they think it is less than 25, they will give a thumbs down. If they think the number of shaded and unshaded dots is about even, they will hold their thumbs sideways.

2. Reveal one square at a time, allowing enough time for students to observe the dots but not enough to count them. After each show of thumbs, ask students to share how they made their estimates. Ask also for estimates of the number of shaded dots.

3. Use Activities 2 and 3 in the same way. Every picture in Activity 2 contains 100 dots; every picture in Activity 3 contains 200 dots.

Solutions

These activities focus on estimation. Exact amounts are given only to facilitate discussion.

Activity 1

1. 25
2. 15
3. 35
4. 5

Activity 2

1. 70
2. 20
3. 65
4. 80

Activity 3

1. 50
2. 100
3. 133

Extending the Activities

● ●

- Tell students the number of shaded dots in each square and have them mentally compute the number of unshaded dots.

- Show collections of small objects of three or more colors and invite estimates of the number of objects of each color in the collection.

About How Many Are Shaded?

Each picture contains 50 dots.

1.

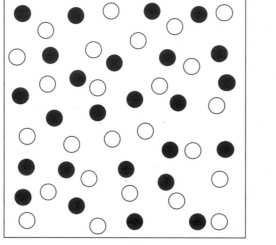

2.

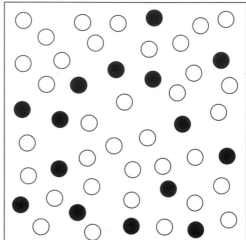

3.

4.

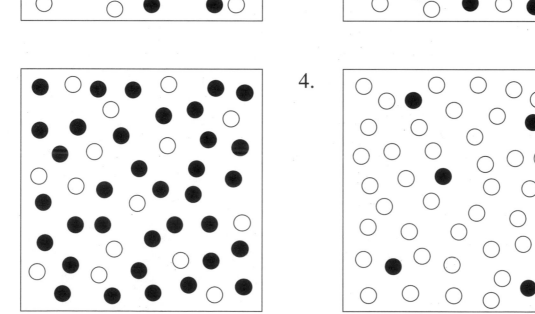

Number SENSE / Grades 3–4

About How Many Are Shaded?

Each picture contains 100 dots.

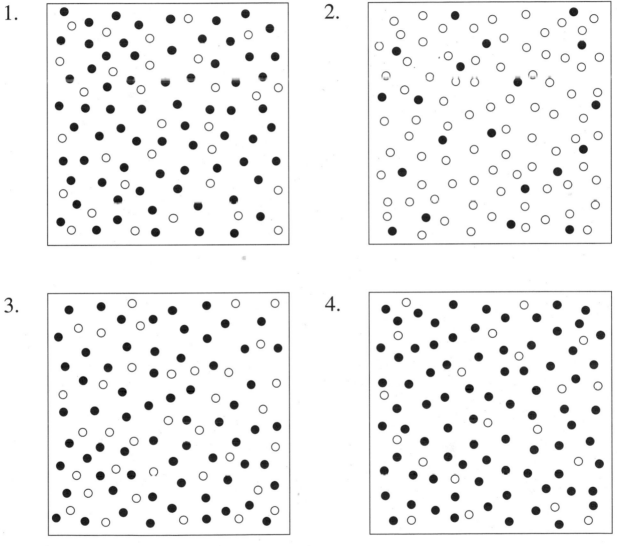

1.

2.

3.

4.

About How Many Are Shaded?

Each picture contains 200 dots.

1.

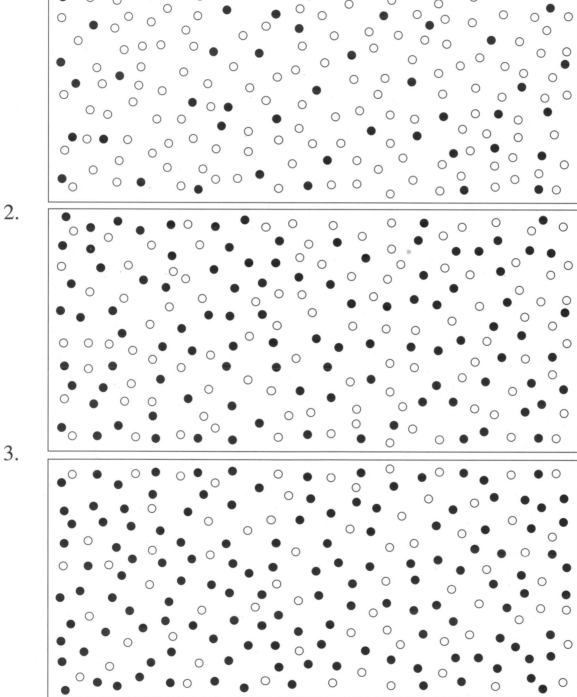

2.

3.

About How Many Do You See?

Number Sense Focus

- Estimation
- Mental computation

Number Focus

- Activities 1–3: Whole numbers

Mathematical Background

If you look at a class of students and think that about 30 students are in the class, the number 30 can serve as a powerful benchmark for estimating the number of people in several classes or in the school. Students need opportunities to learn to use such benchmarks. The goal of estimation is to produce reasonable answers, but what is reasonable depends on the situation. Students must also develop a tolerance for error and learn to recognize when an exact answer may be difficult or impossible to find.

Using the Activities

The value of these activities is the discussion generated as students share how they estimated the numbers of objects in the illustrations.

1. Show the top half of Activity 1 for about 20 seconds, then remove the transparency from view to encourage students to work with the numbers mentally. Ask them to estimate the number of pennies in the collection and to explain how they made their estimates. Make sure they understand that the goal is to give an estimate, not an exact answer.

2. Show the group of 20 pennies on the lower half of the transparency, and ask students to revise their estimates if they wish. Then, ask how knowing the number of pennies in the smaller group influenced their estimate about the number of pennies in the larger collection.

3. Use Activities 2 and 3 in the same way.

Solutions

Encourage and accept all estimates. Here are the actual number of objects.

Activity 1

about 60 pennies

Activity 2

about 300 flies

Activity 3

about 150 books

Extending the Activities

• •

- Ask students to estimate the number of ceiling tiles or floor tiles in the room.

- Have students estimate the number of pages in a book.

- Ask students what other collections of objects they might use as benchmarks in estimating numbers of objects.

About How Many Do You See?

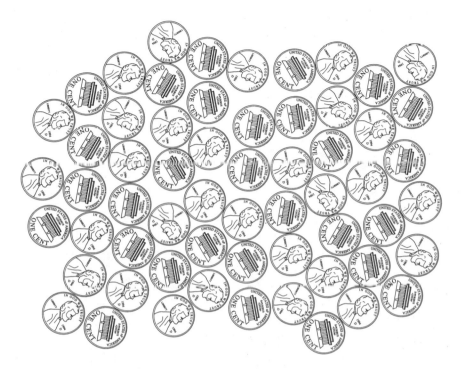

Estimate the number of pennies in this collection.

There are 20 pennies shown below. Now how many pennies do you think are shown above?

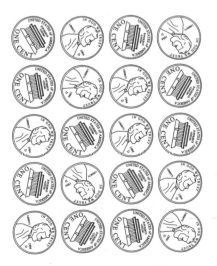

About How Many Do You See?

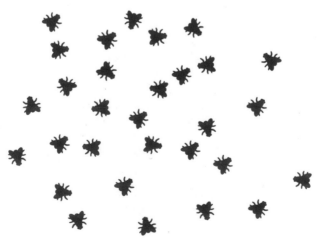

Estimate the number of flies in this swarm. Explain your strategy.

There are 30 flies below. Now how many do you think are in the swarm above?

Number SENSE / Grades 3–4

About How Many Do You See?

Estimate the number of books in this bookcase.

There are 50 books shown below. Now how many do you think are in the bookcase?

EXPERIENCE 31

....

About How Many Will Fit?

Number Sense Focus

- Estimation

Number Focus

- Activities 1–3: Whole numbers

Mathematical Background

....

Part of good number sense is the ability to compare the relative sizes of objects and to quantify that relationship.

Using the Activities

....

In these activities, students are shown a shape and an object and are asked to estimate how many of the objects will fit inside the shape.

1. To prepare for the activities, you will need to collect enough identical objects to fill the three shapes. Choose any of these objects (or any other convenient objects): base 10 longs, base 10 units, any type of small cubes, small lids (one size), square tiles, counters, pattern blocks (one shape at a time), coins (one type at a time), thumbtacks, paper clips, dried beans, macaroni.

2. In Activity 1, begin with an object of which about 10 to 20 will fit in the square. Show one object next to the square, and ask students to estimate how many will fit in the square without extending beyond its edges. Ask them to explain their thinking as a class or to discuss their estimates and estimation strategies in pairs. Record the range of estimates offered.

3. Fill the square with the objects (or have a student do it). When the square is about half full, ask if any students wish to revise their estimates.

4. When as many objects as possible have been put in the square, count the total and compare it with the estimates. Place the emphasis on the estimates that are reasonable—perhaps within 20% of the total—rather than on the estimate nearest the total.

5. Choose another object of a different size, and repeat the activity.

6. Use Activities 2 and 3 in the same way, varying the shape and size of the objects.

Extending the Activities

• •

- Have students estimate the number of books that will fit on their desks.

- Ask students to estimate the number of newspaper pages that will cover the classroom floor.

- Ask students how many cubes, books, or other objects will pack into boxes of given sizes.

About How Many Will Fit?

How many objects will fit in the square? How did you decide?

About How Many Will Fit?

How many objects will fit in the circle? How did you decide?

About How Many Will Fit?

How many objects will fit in the maple leaf? How did you decide?

About How Many Are There?

Activity Focus

- Estimation
- Relative size

Number Focus

- Activities 1–2: Whole numbers

Mathematical Background

Students need many opportunities to apply benchmarks in estimating and to develop a tolerance for error.

Using the Activities

These activities will generate rich discussions as students share how they estimated the numbers of objects in the illustrations.

1. Show the first picture in Activity 1 for about 10 seconds, and mention that there are 20 black sheep shown. Cover the picture, and ask students to estimate the total number of sheep, black and white. Are there more than 30? more than 100? Encourage students to explain their reasoning. Emphasize the use of the known number of black sheep in estimating the total number of sheep.

2. Repeat the procedure with each of the other pictures, always focusing on the estimation strategies used rather than who is nearest the exact answer.

3. In the second half of Activity 2, students must consider not only the number of coins but also their relative values.

Solutions

Accept all reasonable estimates. Here are the exact answers.

Activity 1

60 sheep in all; 25 cups and 45 saucers to the right

Activity 2

90 CDs in all; 20 dimes, $2.10

Extending the Activities

• •

- Show students a pile of 10 to 30 coins of different sizes and ask them to estimate the number of coins and their total value.

- Invite students to talk about collections that they use as benchmarks in estimating numbers of objects.

About How Many Are There?

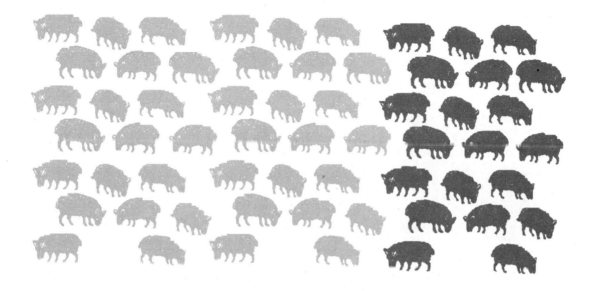

There are 20 black sheep here. About how many sheep are there in all?

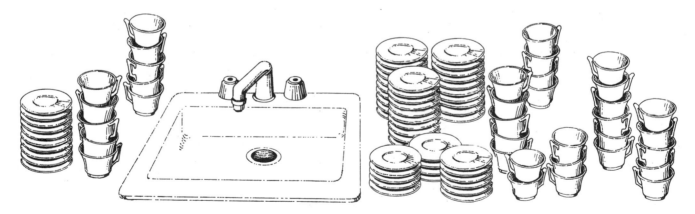

There are 10 cups and 10 saucers to the left of the sink. About how many cups are on the right? About how many saucers are on the right?

About How Many Are There?

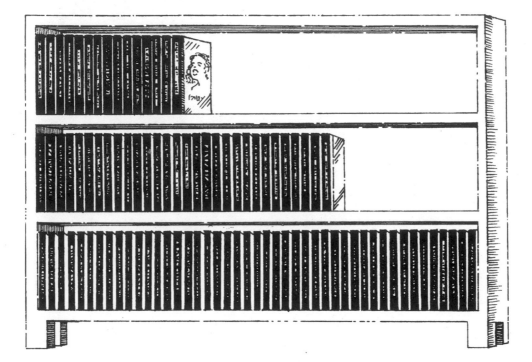

There are 15 CDs on the top shelf. About how many CDs are there in all?

There are 10 pennies shown. About how many dimes are shown?
About how much money is there in all?

Number SENSE / Grades 3–4

About How Many Equals?

Number Sense Focus

- Estimation
- Mental computation

Number Focus

- Activities 1, 2: Whole numbers
- Activity 3: Whole numbers, decimals

Mathematical Background

Connecting counting in multiples with the number of times one number is contained in another will strengthen students' understanding of division and its relation to multiplication. It will also help them acquire strategies for estimating the result of a division.

Using the Activities

In these activities, an overhead calculator will be used to count in multiples of a number. Students will estimate how many times the = button will be pressed before a certain number is reached or exceeded.

1. As a warm-up, display an overhead calculator and press 0 + 2. Ask students to observe what happens as you repeatedly press ⊜ (the display shows 2, 4, 6, 8, . . .). Each time you press ⊜ , stop to ask how many times you have pressed it in all. Encourage students to talk about the connection between the work with the calculator and the mathematics; for example: "I have pressed the button three times" and "3 twos equal 6."

2. Clear the calculator, and key in 0 + 2 again. Ask students how many times you will need to press ⊜ before you reach 8 or more. They should quickly answer that you need to press it four times.

3. In each activity, ask students to estimate the number of times you will press ⊜ before reaching or exceeding the number and to explain their reasons. If they are unsure, encourage them to explain why it will be definitely more or less than a given number of presses.

Extending the Activities

- Have pairs of students work with calculators to construct similar problems for each other.

- Have students choose a number and record its multiples, using the calculator to generate them. Encourage them to look for patterns in the multiples.

- Ask students to experiment with calculators to find numbers whose multiples are easy to estimate—for example, 10, 20, and 100.

About How Many Equals?

Put this in the calculator: 0 + Start Number.

How many times will you press ⎓ before you reach or pass the Goal?

	Start Number	Goal
1.	5	30
2.	5	51
3.	5	77
4.	6	58
5.	6	97
6.	6	115
7.	7	48
8.	7	91
9.	8	65
10.	8	119

About How Many Equals?

Put this in the calculator: 0 + Start Number.
How many times will you press $=$ before you reach or pass the Goal?

	Start Number	Goal
1.	10	60
2.	10	170
3.	10	235
4.	20	60
5.	20	150
6.	30	120
7.	30	200
8.	30	500
9.	25	150
10.	25	325

Number SENSE / Grades 3–4

About How Many Equals?

Put this in the calculator: 0 + Start Number.
How many times will you press ⊜ before you reach or pass the Goal?

	Start Number	Goal
1.	13	50
2.	13	150
3.	13	200
4.	17	100
5.	17	200
6.	17	300
7.	29	200
8.	29	350
9.	0.1	1
10.	0.1	1.8

EXPERIENCE 34

Over or Under?

Number Sense Focus

- Estimation
- Mental computation
- Number relationships

Number Focus

- Activities 1–3: Whole numbers, decimals

Mathematical Background

Discussions about a variety of estimation strategies will help students to develop more efficient and reliable strategies.

Using the Activities

In these activities, students are asked to decide whether the sum of several amounts of money is definitely over, definitely under, or about equal to a given sum.

1. In Activity 1, explain that students do not need to calculate an exact answer but only to decide whether the sum is over, under, or roughly equal to $50. The first question should be obvious to the students.

2. For each sum, encourage students to share their reasoning. In question 3 ($13.66 + $36.48), for example, some students may calculate exactly and say that the sum is definitely over $50; others may reason that $13 and $36 make $49 and that the sum is therefore about $50. Both answers are acceptable, provided they are justified.

3. Use Activities 2 and 3 in the same way.

Extending the Activities

• •

- Have students estimate the cost of two or more items from mail order catalogs and check their estimates with a calculator.

- Have pairs of students start with a target sum, say $100. One student enters a number less than the target into a calculator; the other has 5 seconds to enter an amount that, when added to the first number, produces a total within $5 (or $1) of the target.

Over or Under?

Look at each sum. Is the sum: **Over $50?**   **Under $50?**   **About $50?**

How do you know?

1. $13.21 + $51.43

2. $32.99 + $26.25

3. $13.66 + $36.48

4. $15.37 + $25.95

5. $29.41 + $20.87

6. $15 + $8 + $36

7. $27.24 + $12.75 + $5.98

8. $15.75 + $16.64 + $17.86

9. $25.06 + $3.48 + $27.19

10. $14.47 + $15.94 + $16.26

Number SENSE / Grades 3–4

Over or Under?

Look at each sum. Is the sum: **Over $100? Under $100? About $100?**

How do you know?

1. $54 + $26

2. $28.76 + $81.79

3. $31.45 + $66.85

4. $54.73 + $45.27

5. $14.44 + $84.66

6. $33 + $24 + $51

7. $17.84 + $26.99 + $45.25

8. $33.33 + $33.34 + $33.35

9. $22.46 + $53.18 + $19.58

10. $13.26 + $49.27 + $37.48

Over or Under?

Look at each sum. Is the sum: **Over $150? Under $150? About $150?**

How do you know?

1. $65 + $74

2. $71.69 + $82.14

3. $49.63 + $101.28

4. $47 + $49 + $51

5. $95.65 + $28.47 + $21.63

6. $31.93 + $79.66 + $36.72

7. $19 + $29 + $39 + $49

8. $32 + $57 + $23 + $48

9. $31.14 + $26.52 + $53.28 + $39.17

10. $9.74 + $19.64 + $29.75 + $39.77 + $49.11

Exploring Measurement

Measurement is the context in which adults use numbers most frequently and in which students and adults best learn to make sense of numbers. Among other things, measurement encompasses length, area, volume, capacity, weight, time, and value (such as money). Understanding of the process of measurement and the differing forms and uses of measurement grows in concert with a familiarity with and power over the concept of number.

One's knowledge about measurement begins early and develops over a lifetime. The learning process often involves using standard tools to make direct measurements.

Personal benchmarks promote meaningful comparisons and useful referents, and they help young students develop a sense of numbers and measures. For example:

• "I am 7 years old, and Jean is 8. Jean is taller than I am."

• "My dog is bigger than your dog."

• "Your shoe size is larger than mine."

• "My dad is heavier than my mom."

• "This room is much larger than my bedroom."

• "My beach ball is much bigger than that baseball, but it feels lighter."

The variety of measurement activities in this section will encourage young students to think about numbers and the process of measurement in creative ways. They promote the recognition that all measurement—except the counting of discrete quantities—is *approximate*. Learning to accept that measurements may be close but not exact is the building of a tolerance for error. Such tolerance develops slowly, and students need many experiences with measurement approximation to become comfortable with the concept of error.

Which Is the Longest?

Number Sense Focus

- Measurement
- Relative size

Number Focus

- Activities 1–2: Whole numbers

Mathematical Background

Because line segments can look different depending on one's visual perspective, number lines can be a bewildering model for young students.

Using the Activities

The optical illusions in these activities stimulate careful thinking about number lines and how making accurate measurements might resolve such optical conflicts. In each activity, the line segments shown are of equal length.

1. In Activity 1, show the lines at the top and ask: Are these three horizontal lines the same length? If not, which is the longest? the shortest? Ask students to defend their answers. You might tell them that line A is 8 centimeters long and ask them to estimate the length of lines B and C. Allow students to measure the horizontal segments to confirm that they are of equal length. If the projection of the lines os distorted, don't use the projection to measure. Ask why the segments appear to be different lengths.

2. Show the art at the bottom and ask students to decide which line is longer. You might offer that the vertical line is 10 cm long and ask for an estimate of the horizontal line. Most people estimate the horizontal line as less than 10 cm long. Project the image on a surface, and let students measure the lines. Ask why the lines appear to be different lengths.

3. In Activity 2, ask: Which line is the longest? the shortest? State that line E is 10 centimeters long, and ask students to estimate the length of the longest line. Let students measure the lines, and ask why the lines appear to be different lengths.

Extending the Activities

• Allow students to create their own optical illusions by drawing lines on grid paper.

• Present more optical illusions, such as those in *Can You Believe Your Eyes?* (New York: Brunner/Mazel, 1992) and *Visual Illusion Card Decks* by J. R. Block and H. E. Yuker and *An Optical Slide Show* by T. Pappas (all available from Dale Seymour Publications).

Which Is the Longest?

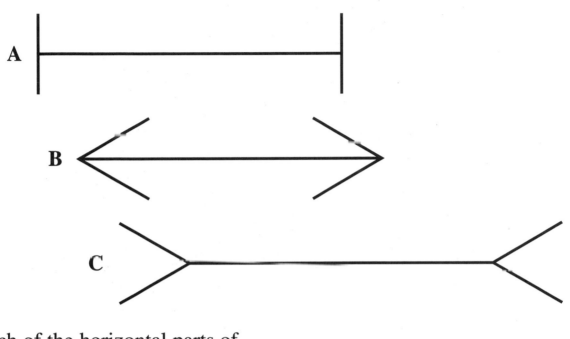

Which of the horizontal parts of
these lines is the longest?

Which is longer, the horizontal line
or the vertical line?

Which Is the Longest?

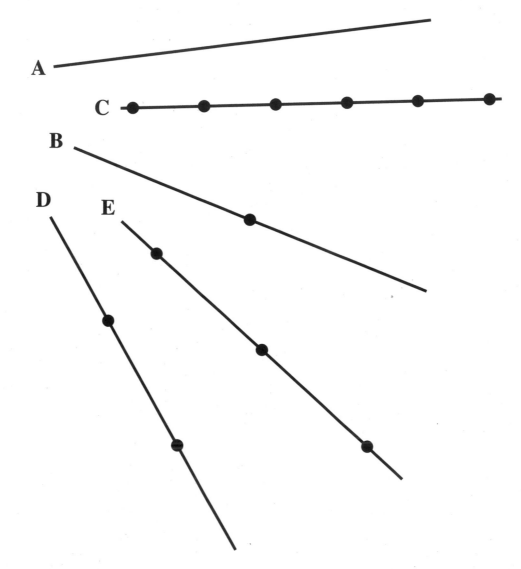

Which of these lines is longest?

. . . .

Using Personal Benchmarks

Number Sense Focus

- Measurement
- Estimation

Number Focus

- Activities 1–3: Whole numbers

Mathematical Background
. . . .

Benchmarks can be used in conjunction with operations such as addition and multiplication to make estimates.

Using the Activities
. . . .

These activities will encourage students to make estimates and to think about and establish bounds as they estimate. Students will need string and scissors for Activity 1.

1. In Activity 1, help the class choose any three of the given distances to estimate, using your height as the unit of measure. (Don't tell students your height!) Have students work in groups to estimate how many teacher heights each distance is.

2. After groups have recorded their estimates, let them cut lengths of string equal to your height and use them to measure and record each distance. Then, help the class compare their estimates to their measurements. Ask questions to extend their thinking:

   - Are all the pieces of string the same length? How do you know? How does this affect your measurements?

   - Which distance did you estimate would be the longest (shortest)? Did it have the longest (shortest) actual measurement?

3. In Activities 2 and 3, students employ personal benchmarks to estimate lengths. Encourage them to use whatever units (inches or feet, centimeters or meters) they wish. As a class, talk about which benchmarks they used to make a particular estimate.

Extending the Activities

• •

- Ask students when "teacher height" would *not* be a useful unit with which to measure.

Using Personal Benchmarks

About how many teacher heights are these things?

- The length of the classroom

- The width of the classroom

- The width of the hall

- The length of the hall

- The distance from the classroom door to the nearest water fountain

- The distance from the classroom door to the office

- The distance from the classroom door to the cafeteria

- The distance from the classroom door to the playground

Using Personal Benchmarks

Here are two fourth graders with their dog.
Estimate the height of these things.

- The girl

- The boy

- The dog

- The wheelchair's largest wheel

- The mailbox

- The stoplight

Using Personal Benchmarks

Here is a third grader relaxing after school. Estimate these things.

- The length of the bed
- The length of the room
- The width of the poster
- The width of the desk
- The height of the closet door
- The width of the bookcase
- The length of the toy airplane

EXPERIENCE 37

How Much Does It Hold?

Number Sense Focus

- Measurement
- Estimation

Number Focus

- Activity 1: Whole numbers

Mathematical Background

Judging the capacity of containers of different sizes and shapes requires a grasp of the concept of conservation of quantity, which develops with experience and maturity. A familiarity with common units of capacity—such as a cup, quart, and gallon—is also useful, as they serve as benchmarks for judging the capacity of nonstandard containers.

Using the Activity

In this experience, students judge the relative sizes of containers and employ appropriate benchmarks.

1. To prepare for the experience, collect five to eight bottles and jars of varying shapes and sizes, ranging from 2 cups to 1 gallon, including one with a capacity of 1 quart. Remove any labels and add an identifying letter (A, B, C, . . .) to each. You will also need a 1-cup measuring cup and access to water.

2. Arrange the containers on a table so the class can see them. Ask: Which bottle do you think holds the most (least) water?

3. Explain that one of the containers holds 1 quart of liquid. Ask students to think about which container it might be. Pose questions to stimulate their thinking:

- How much is a quart?

- What kinds of things come in a quart-size container?

- How can we identify which bottle holds 1 quart?

- Suppose we use a measuring cup to fill the bottle. How many cups make a quart?

Check the students' ideas by pouring 4 cups of water into the containers they choose.

4. Once the quart bottle is identified, ask students to name the containers they think will hold more than a quart and those that will hold less than a quart. Arrange the containers into two groups according to the class's predictions. Let students test their predictions by pouring water from the quart container into the other containers.

5. Use Activity 1 as a follow-up to the work with the real containers.

Extending the Activity

- Allow small groups of students to estimate the order of all the containers by capacity. They can record their estimated order, then experiment by filling the containers with water and making comparisons.

How Much Does It Hold?

For each set of containers:

- Which container probably holds the most?

- Which holds 1 quart? Which holds more than 1 quart?

- Which are you sure holds less than a quart?

Order the containers in each set by how much each holds.

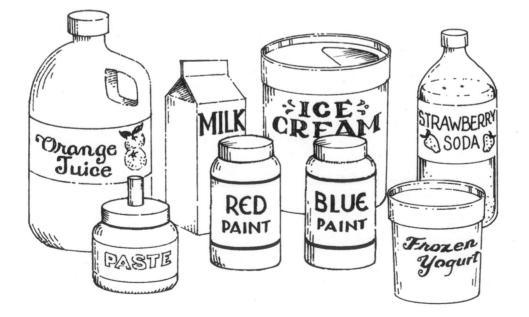

More or Less?

Number Sense Focus

- Measurement
- Estimation

Number Focus

- Activity 1: Whole numbers

Mathematical Background

Benchmarks are a cornerstone of measurement and estimation. Once benchmarks are identified and internalized, they can be used to make estimates.

Using the Activity

This activity will encourage students to make estimates using benchmarks and to think about and establish bounds as they estimate.

1. Have students work in groups to estimate the number of units (such as feet, strides, arm lengths, centimeters, or meters) it is across something (such as a desk, a door, or the classroom). As they work, ask them to decide the following:

   - The distance is definitely more than _____ units.

   - The distance is definitely less than _____ units.

   Emphasize that students should not choose upper or lower bounds that they think might not be correct, but bounds they are certain contain the actual length.

2. When all groups have had enough time to choose their bounds, record them on the board in a chart:

Group	A	B	C	D
Definitely More Than	50 cm	90 cm	80 cm	50 cm
Definitely Less Than	150 cm	120 cm	200 cm	100 cm

3. Ask groups to describe their strategies for deciding on the upper and lower bounds. Discuss which strategies they think are most efficient. Which groups have very narrow bounds? very wide bounds?

4. Ask whether all the groups could be correct (yes, in this case, provided the length is between 90 cm and 100 cm).

5. As a class, find the actual measurement. Talk about possible explanations for any incorrect bounds.

6. Use the transparency for Activity 1 to encourage students to think about reasonable bounds for actual measurements.

Extending the Activity

• •

- Present other measuring challenges, such as:
  - What is the area of the ceiling?
  - What is the weight of your math book?
  - What is the capacity of this container?
  - How many words are on this page?
  - How many marbles are in this jar?

- Invite groups of students to present similar challenges.

More or Less?

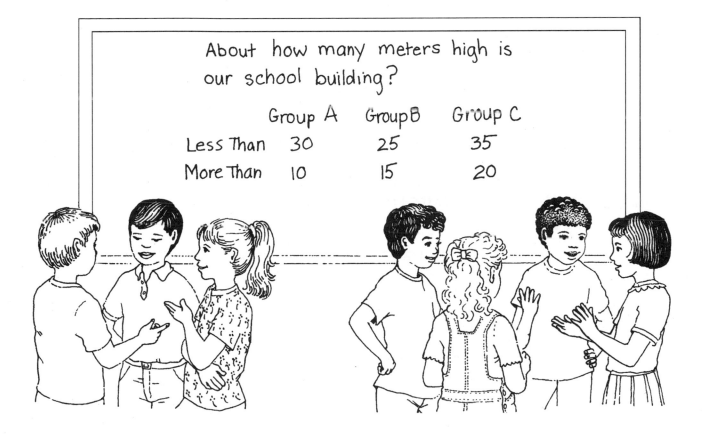

About how many meters high is our school building?

	Group A	Group B	Group C
Less Than	30	25	35
More Than	10	15	20

Think about these measurements.

- How many steps is it from the door of the classroom to the nearest drinking fountain?

- How many of our math books will it take to make a stack as high as the teacher's desk?

- How many meter sticks would it take to go around the school property?

- How many oranges would it take to fill the cafeteria?

EXPERIENCE 39

• •

Who Gets to Go?

Number Sense Focus

- Measurement
- Relative size
- Reasonableness

Number Focus

- Activities 1–3: Whole numbers

Mathematical Background

• •

Units of time are everyday measurements that employ personal benchmarks and have direct connections to mathematics.

Using the Activities

• •

These activities will help students establish meaningful relationships among measurements of time and apply them to real-life situations.

1. Students often measure time by such personal benchmarks as their grade level and birthday. "My birthday is two days before yours, so I'm older." As a warm-up, ask each student to find someone in class who is older and someone in class who is younger than they are. Then, explore these questions:

    - Can everyone find someone younger? Why? *(No, because there must be a youngest student in the class.)*

    - Can everyone find someone older? Why? *(No, because there must be an oldest student.)*

2. In Activity 1, show the illustration, and make sure students know "today's date" and the age required to see the movie. Then, ask which students in the given class are allowed to attend. Students should realize that the ages listed are for the previous September. If they are having trouble, ask clarifying questions:

- Who is the oldest student in this class? Who is the youngest?

- Suppose another student, Sally, is older than Kelly but younger than Marcelo. What could Sally's birthday be?

- Who is younger than Sara?

- Which students were born in the same year?

3. Activities 2 and 3 explore other real-life applications of measurement. In Activity 2, make sure students realize that the date is January 1. You may want to raise the question of exact time of birth: should Bo have to buy an adult's ticket if he is visiting the aquarium in the morning but was born in the evening?

Solutions

Activity 1

Drew, Marcelo, Meela, Sara, and Sascha

Activity 2

Daryl, Mai, and Bo

Activity 3

Katie, Lawrence, Yvonne, Josh, Yoko, and Rubin

Extending the Activities

• •

- Ask students to describe other situations in which a measurement such as age or height is used to determine eligibility.

- Pose this question: Is it possible for twins to have different birthdays?

Who Gets to Go?

Class List

Name	Age September 1	Birthday
Drew	9	September 20
Carol	9	February 14
Marcelo	10	November 5
Kelly	9	January 28
Meela	10	May 1
Sara	9	January 23
Sascha	9	December 25

Who is old enough to see the movie?

Who Gets to Go?

Class List

Name	Age September 1	Birthday
Daryl	10	September 20
Carl	10	February 14
Mai	11	November 5
Kalama	10	January 2
Kim	10	May 1
Trish	9	January 23
Carlos	9	December 31
Bo	10	January 1

Who needs an adult's ticket?

Who Gets to Go?

To Ride the *Giant Dipper*

You must be at least 139 cm tall
or at least 38 kg
or at least 11 years old.

Name	Age	Height in centimeters	Mass in kilograms
Luisa	10	135	34
Katie	10	142	32
Lawrence	11	130	30
Yvonne	10	151	35
Josh	10	140	37
Yoko	9	135	39
Rubin	9	139	41
Hani	10	129	30

Who is allowed to ride the Giant Dipper?

Number SENSE / Grades 3–4

Numbers on a Line

Number Sense Focus

- Measurement
- Estimation

Number Focus

- Activity 1: Whole numbers

Mathematical Background

The number line is a valuable model for representing the size and order of numbers. Students will become more comfortable with the number line as they use it.

Using the Activity

1. For this activity, you will need an 8-foot length of string, 10 to 15 clothespins, and a set of index cards with one number on each, from 0 to 300 in multiples of 10. Stretch the string across the front of the room like a clothesline, perhaps along the chalkboard. Place the 0 and 300 cards at the ends of the line using clothespins. Distribute the remaining number cards to the students.

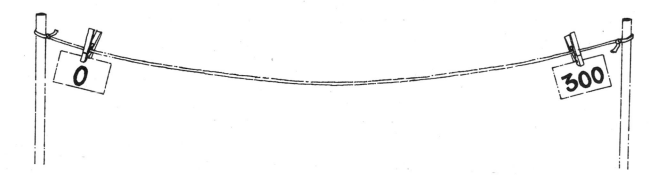

2. Point to the center of the string (halfway between 0 and 300) and ask someone to name the number this point represents. Have the student holding 150 hang the card on the line. Point slightly to the left of 150, and ask what number might go there. Several answers may be suggested (such as 120, 130, or 140). Accept whatever suggestion the students feel most comfortable with, and remind them that they can adjust the positions of cards later. Ask other students to hang their numbers as the class locates their positions. Focus on reasonable rather than exact locations. Encourage students to explain their thinking, emphasizing the use of terms such as *between, more than,* and *less than.*

3. Follow this discussion with Activity 1. If necessary, use the clothesline model to help students find the values of the blank cards.

4. The number line in part 4 shows only a single benchmark of 100, so the value of the cards depends on the scale. The line could go from 90 to 110, from 0 to 200, or some other range. There is no best answer; any values satisfying the conditions are correct. Encourage students to explain their answers.

Extending the Activity

• Repeat the activity—using either the physical model or a sketch—with other endpoints, such as 50 and 150 or 0 and 3000.

Numbers on a Line

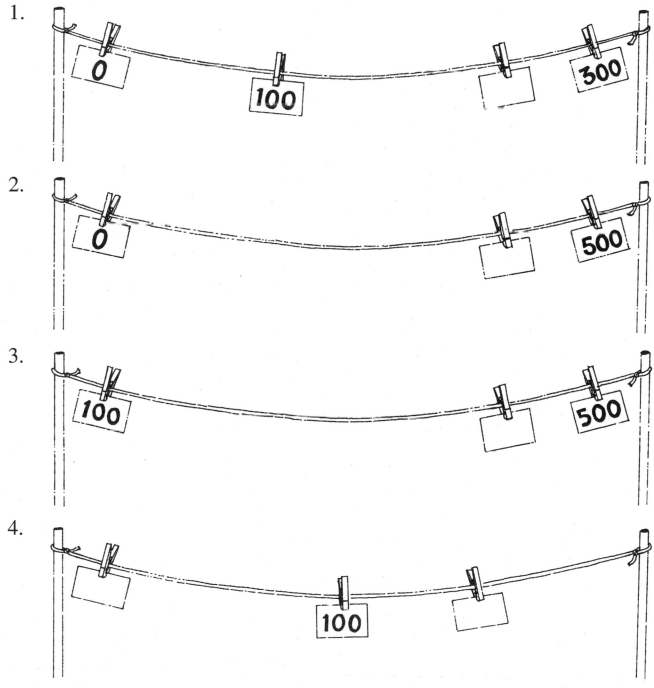

1.

2.

3.

4.

Estimate the value of each blank number card.

EXPERIENCE 41

Time Out

Number Sense Focus

- Measurement
- Relative size
- Multiple representation
- Reasonableness

Number Focus

- Activities 1–3: Whole numbers

Mathematical Background

Concepts involving units of time—seconds, minutes, hours, days, weeks, months, years, leap years, decades, centuries—develop slowly. Some of these units make useful benchmarks, and each is related to the others.

Using the Activities

These activities encourage students to reflect upon and to use units of time.

1. Students often measure time with personal benchmarks, such as their grade, their birthday, and special or disturbing events. As a warm-up, ask students to share three things that happened

   - before they came to school today

   - after they came to school today

   - before their birth

   - after their birth

   List the events that are mentioned. Talk about the idea that such categories are helpful for placing events in time.

2. Activity 1 asks students to place personal events into different time frames. As you make each list, encourage students to share how they know an event belongs in a particular time category.

3. In Activity 2, the focus is on approximate or reasonable answers. For example, 100 seconds is almost 2 minutes, and the 100th day of the year always falls in April.

4. Activity 3 begins with a question about how many days students have lived, an idea that is challenging for students of all ages. Students often feel they have lived a long time, and most associate this feeling with a large number of days. Encourage students to think about the question, do some estimation, and then choose the best answer. Survey them about their decisions and their reasoning. Research shows that less than half of students in grades 3 and 4 answer this question correctly, and most choose much larger values. Talking about these questions will help students realize that 4000 days is about 10 years, but 40,000 days is over 100 years and 400,000 days is over 1000 years! This is a good opportunity for students to use calculators to explore these and related relationships.

Solutions

Activity 2

1. 2   2. 2   3. 4   4. 3   5. 2

Activity 3

1. 4000   2. yes   3. yes   4. no   5. yes   6. no

Extending the Activities

• •

- Ask students: About how many days are in a decade? a century? In what year will you be a decade old? a century old?

- Challenge students to figure out when they were 1000 days old and 2000 days old.

- Ask students to make a list of people (parents, teachers, grandparents) they know who have lived 10,000 (20,000) days.

Time Out

Name three things that happened:

Today   Yesterday

This week   Last week

This month   Last month

This year   Last year

Time Out

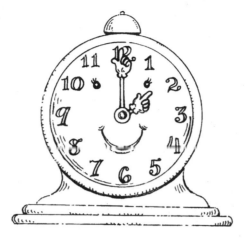

1. 100 seconds is about _____ minutes.

2. 100 minutes is about _____ hours.

3. 100 hours is about _____ days.

4. 100 days is about _____ months.

5. 100 weeks is about _____ years.

Time Out

1. About how many days have you lived?

   400   4000   40,000   400,000   4,000,000

2. Are there more than 1000 seconds in a day?

3. Are there more than 1000 minutes in a day?

4. Are there more than a 1000 hours in a month?

5. Have you lived 1000 days?

6. Have you lived 1000 weeks?